By Kitty Plunkett

**Design by
Edward A. Conner**

**Donning Company/
Publishers
Norfolk, Virginia**

A view of Main Street in 1888,
looking north from Court.

Courtesy of Memphis Room, MASPLIC

Memphis A PICTORIAL HISTORY

Library of Congress Cataloging in Publication Data:

Plunkett, Kitty, 1946-
Memphis, a pictorial history.
1. Memphis—History—Pictorial works.
2. Memphis—Description—Views. I. Title.
F444.M5P58   976.8'19   76-54971
ISBN 0-915442-24-8

Printed in the United States of America

Excerpt from the song "Bring Back Beale Street" is
included with the permission of the author, Danny
Thomas.

Telephone wires are visible running from the wharf
boat to poles on shore. Around the turn of the
century, permanent wharf boats supplied the
riverboats with everything they needed. Later, they
were replaced by small boats that met the barges right
on the river and supplied them with food, fuel and
fresh crews.

Courtesy of Bert Odessa Wade

To Mike, Donna and Bob

Children waded into the Wolf River at Raleigh
Springs for this picture, taken around 1900.

Courtesy of Henry Frank

INTRODUCTION

Memphis: A Pictorial History depicts a town viewed by the sophisticated photographer, its images burned on sensitive film, developed, selected, enlarged by the artist using ever more precise equipment. And it is a record by the untrained hand of the amateur capturing his most important moments with his trusty magic black box. It traces photography's progress along with the city's, beginning when the photographic subject had to stay completely still not to blur his image and when Memphis was a bawdy, fervent, vigorous river town that wouldn't hold still for anything.

The book doesn't pretend to be complete in historical detail. Happenstance made its photo selections before I did and scattered what it didn't destroy. But the pictures that did survive tell the story of Memphis from the Civil War and river life to its phenomenal growth and opulence and reverence for cotton. They provide a sketch of Memphis history and in several instances they serve as a departure point for the thousand words needed to tell a story one picture could have told had it survived. Probably many of the pictures in my head were never taken. As many Memphians have told me, a way of life seems ordinary until it's gone. You don't need a picture of the roustabouts heaving cotton when you can go down there every Saturday and watch 'em. And Beale Street? It so teemed with life nobody imagined it would die.

Although chronology was important in determining the order of the book, story sense had the final say. The river pictures, for instance, covering the early days of showboats up through the excursion boats and tugs of the mid-twentieth century, are grouped together in the 1880s and 1890s, in the days of Jim Lee and river races and loading a boat with cotton till she threatened to sink.

In instances where an address is given in the caption of a picture, the numbers have been left off to avoid confusion. Before 1905, houses and buildings in Memphis were numbered randomly. In that year, thoroughfares running north and south were dubbed street, those running east and west renamed avenue, and numbers were assigned consecutively.

I wish to thank those who generously gave me permission to use their photographs, whose names appear under the captions in this book. Many of them also tutored me in Memphis history and shared their experiences and insights. I also wish to thank James Purdy, Fred Hutchins, Exie Hardamon, George Treadwell, Fred Manton, Lee Winchester, William Gerber, George Hettinger, James Huey, Judge William Leffler, Charles Russell, Nat D. Williams, Aretta Polk, Brother Leo O'Donnell, and the many others who granted interviews and enlightened my subject. Special thanks to Dale Carr for lending an artistic hand to early maps of Memphis, to Irene Taylor Zinn for diary excerpts, and to Gene Tuck for an excellent job of copying old photographs. Thanks to the staff of the Memphis Room of Memphis and Shelby County Public Library and Information Center (MASPLIC) and to Brier Smith of the Memphis Pink Palace Museum. I am deeply grateful to Stephen Findlay, Thomas Rhodes, Edward F. Williams, III, Dr. F. Jack Hurley, Eleanor D. Hughes, and Dr. James E. Roper for reading the manuscript and providing invaluable suggestions and professional advice.

Kitty Plunkett
Memphis, 1976

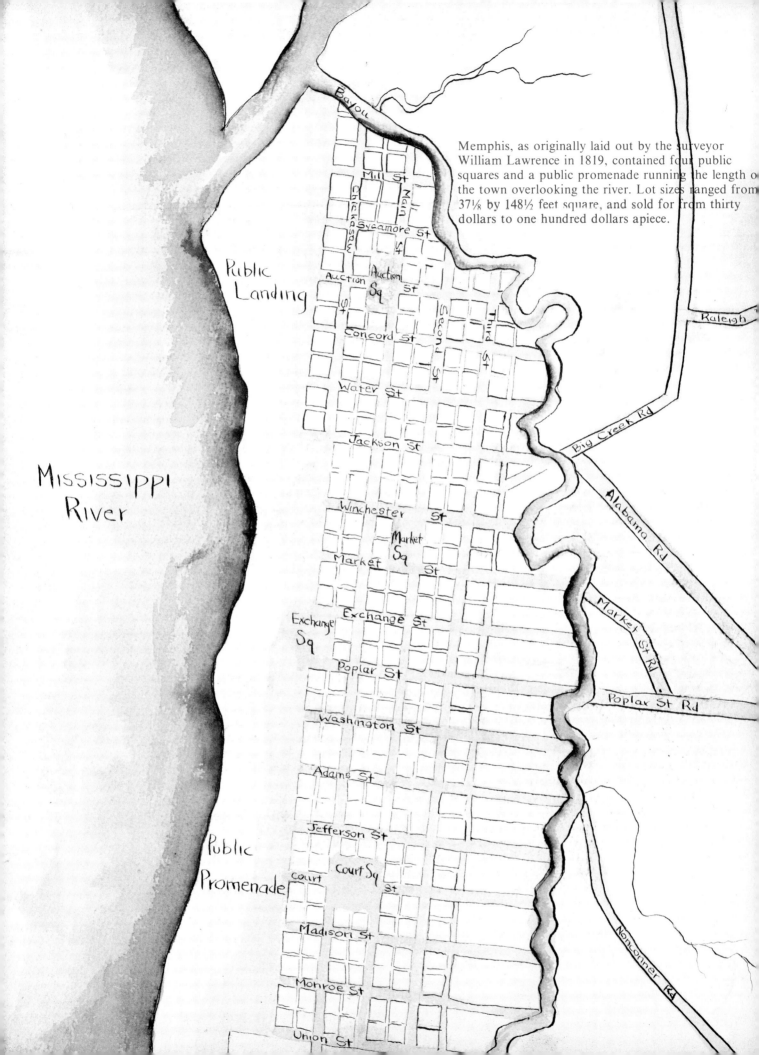

Memphis, as originally laid out by the surveyor William Lawrence in 1819, contained four public squares and a public promenade running the length of the town overlooking the river. Lot sizes ranged from 37⅛ by 148½ feet square, and sold for from thirty dollars to one hundred dollars apiece.

Mississippi River

Public Landing

Public Promenade

Bayou

Mill St

Main St

Chickasaw St

Sycamore St

Auction Sq

Auction St

Second St

Third St

Concord St

Water St

Jackson St

Winchester St

Market Sq

Market St

Exchange St

Exchange Sq

Poplar St

Washington St

Adams St

Jefferson St

Court Sq

Court St

Madison St

Monroe St

Union St

Raleigh

Big Creek Rd

Alabama Rd

Market St Rd

Poplar St Rd

Nonconner Rd

1541-1819

On December 15, 1811, rumblings along the New
Madrid Fault began. In the next thirteen weeks the
crack in the earth paralleling the Mississippi from
southern Illinois to Arkansas shifted 1,874 times. The
land quaked, trees were felled and the mighty river
rushed into virgin fields at the behest of tremors of
the highest measurable degree. The few people
huddled at the frontier post on the bluff above the
Mississippi trembled in fear. Then all was quiet.

The resultant topographical changes cast doubt
on whether the exact site of Memphis was visited by
early explorers of the Mississippi, because the
recorded descriptions don't quite fit the land anymore.
But supposedly the Spaniard Hernando de Soto
crossed the Mississippi near Memphis in 1541. In the
next century, Louis Joliet and Jacques Marquette may
have stopped on their way down the Mississippi in
search of a route to the Pacific. In 1682, a member of
La Salle's party was lost while hunting and his
companions built a fort on a bluff near Memphis and
named it for the lost man, Pierre Prudhomme. Half a
century later, the French governor of Louisiana, Sieur
Jean Baptiste Lemoyne de Bienville, built Fort
Assumption on the "Heights of Prudhomme." It is
Memphis' first known recorded historical fact, dated
1739.

While foreign explorers were charting new lands,
the Chickasaw Indians continued to hunt on the
river bluffs as they had done for generations.
They did business at the trading post and made
war with the Spanish and French until 1818, when

The Old Bell Tavern, built sometime in the 1820s, was originally a store that sold whiskey and tobacco. It stood on the east side of Front Street and was bought by Paddy Meagher and turned into a tavern in 1823. It had no sign other than a large bell hung in front of the door. This picture was made shortly before the building was demolished in the early 1900s. Reportedly, after the death of Paddy Meagher, the tavern acquired a bad reputation.

Courtesy of Memphis Room, MASPLIC

1819-1839

Two land speculators in the 1790s obtained rights to a tract of land in the Western District originally purchased by a North Carolinian named John Rice. Nearly three decades later, after the Chickasaw Indians ceded their land rights in the area, they acquired a new partner, surveyed the five thousand acres, and marked off lots for a town. One partner, General Andrew Jackson, sold his interest to John McLemore and went on to become President of the United States. Another, retired Tennessee Supreme Court Justice John Overton, nurtured his growth and it made his fortune. The third, General James Winchester, sired its first mayor and named the town Memphis after the ancient Egyptian city south of Cairo on the Nile. Egyptian scholars have defined Memphis as meaning "white walls" or "glory of men," but to Memphians it has always been "place of good abode." The original source of the definition is unknown.

Judge Overton persuaded the State Legislature to make Shelby—named for the Indian agent and Revolutionary War hero Isaac Shelby—a county. It was the first to be entirely within the Western District. Soon a small town grew and its inhabitants lived by barter with Indians and flatboatmen. The new city was granted a charter of incorporation in 1826. Above protest from Memphians, the county seat had been relocated at Sanderlin's Bluff in 1824 and the town of Raleigh laid out. Raleigh soon surpassed Memphis in population and refinement, for Memphis was a rough and brawling river town, periodically lawless when the boatmen landed. Even as a river town it had its rivals, for the Mississippi continually changed and water favorable to docking determined where the boats would put in and where trade would flourish. South Memphis, Fort Pickering, and Randolph at different times threatened to surpass Memphis in river business.

In this period the first major outbreaks of disease occurred. In 1826 and 1832 there were cholera epidemics, and in 1828, yellow fever, which in its later manifestations would nearly destroy the city.

During the 1820s, carts and wagons were heading west in droves and many little towns were settled. Even with competition of other towns, its unhealthful reputation and its bawdiness, Memphis grew. Its first cotton shipment came by wagon from Fayette County

in 1826, and by 1834 it had its own line of packets. Its citizens were of many nationalities. There was a newspaper by 1827 and the Farmers & Merchants Bank was founded in 1832. From a handful in 1819, Memphis grew to almost 1,800 in 1839. As the future meeting place of the Mississippi River and the rails from the East, she was destined to outdistance her rivals within a few decades.

Calvary Episcopal Church at North Second Street was founded in 1832 by the first area Episcopal clergyman, the Reverend Thomas Wright. The building, erected in the mid-1840s, is one of the oldest public buildings in Memphis.

Courtesy of Memphis Area Chamber of Commerce

Rawlings Trading Post, built by the area's first known permanent white settler, Ike Rawlings, was established at Fort Pickering in 1813, six years before the town of Memphis was laid out. He set up shop in Memphis in 1821. His business quickly grew with the town, from a trading post to a general store. He became a community leader and was elected mayor in 1829. This building stood on the west side of Second, between Jackson and Winchester Streets, and fronted an alley in the original plat of the town. Rawlings requested that the alley be widened and he named it Commerce Street. The building was still standing when *The History of the City of Memphis* by James Davis was written in 1873, but the hill on which it stood had been graded and the basement had become the first story of the building.

Courtesy of Memphis Room, MASPLIC

The controversial Marcus Brutus Winchester, Memphis' first mayor and postmaster, was the son of General James Winchester, one of the founders. He resigned as mayor when a law was enacted in 1829 making it illegal for one man to hold both positions, and Ike Rawlings was elected. However, he continued in a position of leadership, as a financial expert, merchant, and postmaster, and was elected to a seat in the State Legislature in 1851.

Many early settlers were against Winchester because he represented the landowners. He further raised their ire by associating with Frances Wright, the Scotswoman who founded the unsuccessful Nashoba community at Germantown for the emancipation of slaves. After his marriage to a beautiful French quadroon, he and his family were socially ostracized. Although Marcus was treated with respect in his business dealings and esteemed by many, at one point citizens attempted to drive him out of town.

Courtesy of Memphis Pink Palace Museum

Eugene Magevney came to Memphis from County Fermanagh, Ireland, in 1833 and was one of the town's first schoolteachers. His house, on Adams Avenue, was given to the city by his descendants and is now operated as part of the Memphis Pink Palace Museum. The first Catholic marriage in Memphis was performed in the house after Eugene sent to Ireland for his fiancee Mary Smyth in 1840. This recent photo shows the rear of the house and gardens.

Courtesy of Memphis Room, MASPLIC

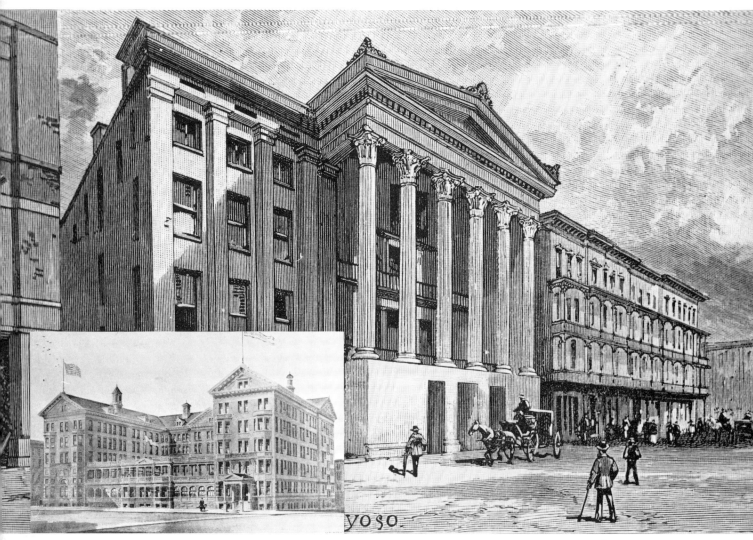

yoso.

When the Gayoso House opened in the 1840s, some said it was more magnificent than any hotel in New York City. They also found such elegance incongruous with the density of the surrounding forest and the smallness of the nearby river towns. As Daniel J. Boorstin wrote in *The Americans: The National Experience*, "By a homeopathic magic, such a hotel was supposed to make the city grow. Somehow Memphis would become a cotton capital because it already had a public palace worthy of one." The Gayoso was a bit ahead of its time, but it was soon filled with planters and their families stopping over on their way to the springs at Raleigh, and it served the Nashville Stage. Its builder, Robertson Topp, had provided Memphis a magnificent backdrop for many historical events. It was over this hotel the Confederate flag was raised when Memphis was eager for secession, and it was the headquarters of General Gideon Pillow. Reportedly Bill Forrest and his men rode into the lobby on horseback to capture General Hurlbut when the city was under the control of the Federals.

The hotel was destroyed by fire in 1899. On the same site a new Hotel Gayoso (see inset) was erected. Until the Peabody was built in 1924, the Gayoso remained Memphis' finest. Goldsmith's department store bought the hotel in 1948 and converted part of it into offices. In 1962, the Gayoso closed for good. Goldsmith's now holds conferences in the room that came to be known as Bob Hope's suite. The finery has been replaced by a long meeting table.

Courtesy of Memphis Room, MASPLIC

1839-1865

America took to photography like steam to the river. The artist Louis Daguerre and the inventor Joseph Niepce, both Frenchmen, had found a way to capture the elusive image. Within a year of the revelation of their discovery, Americans had embraced photography and soon daguerreian galleries appeared in every major city. Portraiture was the order of the day. Exposure time was thirty seconds, allowing for no movement, and the equipment was too cumbersome to transport to outdoor locations easily. Modifications of the photographic process were quick to follow. The ambrotype, 1854, made processing faster. The tintype, 1856, was less fragile, and the wet plate process, 1854, with the use of a negative, made possible multiple production of a single print.

In 1850, four daguerreotypists were listed in the Memphis City Directory. Photography was a luxury well afforded by people growing rich from cotton.

Other businesses in Memphis also began to flourish. Corn, wheat, and tobacco were shipped from Memphis, but cotton soon became the most important product. In 1850, West Tennessee was producing more than four-fifths of the state's cotton crop, and at a London exposition, Shelby cotton was judged best in the world.

Memphis still suffered from the exuberance of the river men in the beginning of the 1840s, but Mayor Spickernagle, with the help of a couple of guard groups, challenged them and won, bringing an end to their reign of lawlessness.

In 1841, the populated area of the city was bounded by Poplar on the south. Front Row, along the river, was the principal business district. In 1849, South Memphis, once a bitter rival, voted with Memphis to merge. The first public schools opened in 1848, though buildings to house them were not erected until after the war. Private schools included St. Agnes Academy, 1851, Mr. Whitehorne's Grammar School and the Misses Young's School for Girls. Memphis Female College and State Female College were founded in the 1850s.

Memphis organized its first paid fire company in 1860, and soon gas lamps were installed to illuminate the night streets. In April of 1857, the first train from Charleston arrived in Memphis, linking the Mississippi River and the Atlantic. In 1843, the land bounded by Front Row and the river, Auction and Market Streets, was donated for a United States Navy Yard.

The period was not without its problems. After deciding to improve the streets which were muddy and full of holes, the city wasted money on inadequate improvements and lost further on railroad subscriptions and ended up with a municipal debt of over a million dollars with little to show for it. A board of health was appointed in 1838, and an 1850s newspaper health campaign resulted in the purchase of land for a quarantine station, but in 1855 yellow fever struck again, claiming two hundred and twenty lives.

In 1861, just before the Civil War, Memphis was the sixth largest Southern city. She stood, high on her river bluff, imperfect but proud, little fearing that Yankee hearts would soon covet her river location and her rails.

The Lee home on Adams Avenue, part of the Victorian Village Historic District, was built in 1848 by William Harsson. Additions were made in 1860 and 1871, and it was bought by Captain James Lee, Jr., of the Lee Steamship Lines in 1890. In 1929, Miss Rosa Lee deeded the house to the City of Memphis for use of the Memphis Art Association.

Courtesy of Memphis Housing Authority

This building, which housed the original Memphis Country Club, was built by Geraldus Buntyn before the Civil War. It burned in 1910, and a new building for the club was erected on the site.

Courtesy of Bert Odessa Wade

An Illinois Central steam locomotive in use during the 1860s. It was the classic American locomotive of the nineteenth century.

Courtesy of Memphis Room, MASPLIC

This building was erected on Adams Avenue in 1854 by the Reverend Cornelius G. McPherson to house the Memphis Female College. It operated as such until 1871, when it closed and the Christian Brothers, under Brother Maurelian, bought it for a school. In 1940 the Christian Brothers relocated their schools; in 1964 this building was demolished.

Courtesy of Christian Brothers College

Civil War

From high on the bluffs, June 6, 1862, through the smoke and flames of cannon fire, Memphis witnessed with horror the hour-long river battle that delivered their city to the Federals as prize. With the Confederate vessels sunk or captured and land troops engaged elsewhere, the city was taken with little opposition. The Union flag was raised, beginning three years of occupation.

Memphis had been pro-Union in the beginning. But by the time Sumter fell and Lincoln called for troops, Memphis was wholeheartedly in favor of joining the Confederacy. Tennessee seceded and Memphis promised a thousand men within seven days. Those at home were sure of victory, and in their exuberance named a street Manassas for the victory at Manassas Junction, Virginia.

After her occupation, Memphis was the center of contraband trade, and historians believe the city was more valuable to the Confederacy as an occupied city for that reason. Municipal government was maintained until the last year, when martial law was instituted. For Memphis citizens times were hard. They numbered twenty-two thousand including slaves before the war, but newcomers had swelled the population to thirty-five thousand. Among the newcomers were gamblers, sharpers, and speculators. Prices soared. Every available building was turned into a hospital and anxious wives arrived from great distances to seek their men among the wounded.

Compared to other Southern cities, though, Memphis suffered little from the war. Her buildings were intact and trade had been maintained. Within five years, she had surpassed her pre-war economy.

Before the war, Forrest & Maples owned the largest slave mart in Memphis. A lithograph from a city directory advertisement.

Courtesy of Robert Ledbetter

These veterans of Troop A, Forrest Cavalry, were photographed in Nashville in the late 1800s.

Courtesy of Memphis Room, MASPLIC

Nathan Bedford Forrest emerged as Memphis' hero of the Civil War. When this picture was taken, Forrest was an alderman. Described as near-illiterate but energetic, intelligent, and courageous, he made money in horse trading, real estate, and slave trading, then retired in 1859 to become a planter. In the Civil War he rose from the rank of private to lieutenant general, the only soldier in American history to accomplish that feat in a single war. After serving under Bragg, he was reassigned to North Mississippi to form Forrest Cavalry Corps, whose clever and daring feats became legendary. In his famous raid on occupied Memphis, he succeeded in diverting the Union Army from its march on Oxford, and won the admiration of Memphians who watched his surprise attack with unconcealed delight. After the war he was named president of the Memphis & Selma Railroad and became grand wizard of the Ku Klux Klan.

Courtesy of Memphis Pink Palace Museum

The Union fleet, consisting of four ironclads and four rams, two miles above Memphis in preparation for battle. This photograph was taken June 5, 1862. The eyewitness account of Mrs. S. C. Toof relates that early the next morning the Confederate gunboats fired the first shot, then the Yankee boats rapidly advanced. They seemed to join hands, she wrote, and their cannon balls and bullets flew in every direction accompanied by the screams of the people watching from the bluff.

*From **The Photographic History of the Civil War***

The *Cairo*, one of seven flat-bottomed stern-wheelers constructed by the Union after the war broke out. It had three guns on the front and four on each broadside. It was 175 feet long, its sloping sides two feet thick.

*From **The Photographic History of the Civil War***

This rare photograph of the inspection of Union soldiers during Memphis' occupation was taken by a Main Street photographer named H. A. Balch, June 10, 1865. The businesses behind the barracks buildings on Front Street are C. Mengel & Co., wholesale tobacco; A. P. Burditt & Co., wholesale grocers and cotton factors; Wolcott & Swasey; Orgill Brothers, wholesale hardware; A. P. Moore of Silvey, Moore & Co.; and J. G. Wallace, grocers and commission merchants.

Orgill Brothers, still run by the original family in the 1970s, was founded in 1850. It had an iron shop in a shed at the rear. Orgill Brothers occupied the same site on Front Street until 1922.

Courtesy of Herb Peck, Jr.

A detail of the previous photograph.

Courtesy of Herb Peck, Jr.

Men of McClernand's troops in Memphis prior to
Federal occupation.

*From **The Photographic History of the Civil War***

The Memphis & Charleston Railroad yards in the
1860s. The Memphis & Charleston Depot was located
on Lauderdale, now Danny Thomas Boulevard.
Completed in 1857, it was the first east-west rail route
to Memphis. After the Battle of Shiloh, the railroad
fell into Union hands. The line was later absorbed by
the Southern.

Courtesy of Memphis Room, MASPLIC

Private John Rulle, a Confederate soldier from Memphis, was attached to Company "K," Second Tennessee Infantry.

Courtesy of Herb Peck, Jr.

A daguerreotype of Captain C. H. Watkins, carrying a Memphis made Leech & Rigdon sword. The firm operated under the name Memphis Novelty Works and made Confederate swords under contract. When Memphis fell in 1862, the company moved to Columbus, Mississippi, and then, in December, moved to Georgia. They were always one step ahead of the Union soldiers. During this period they continued to make swords, bayonets, and spurs, and began manufacturing revolvers. The swords, issued to enlisted men, were ornate brass with the letters "CS" surrounded by tobacco leaves and floral decorations. The owner's initials were etched on the blade; the scabbard was black leather with brass mountings.

Courtesy of Dr. Roland Bill

A daguerreotype of a corporal and private in the Union Army during Memphis' occupation. The pistol held by the man on the left was nicknamed the suicide special because it had an exposed trigger.

Courtesy of Dr. Roland Bill

The Hunt-Phelan home, Beale Street, was General Grant's Memphis headquarters, though he usually slept in a tent under one of the elms. In its library, Grant planned the Vicksburg campaign. Between 1863 and 1865, thousands of Union soldiers stayed here. A barracks building was erected on the lawn to serve as a hospital. After the war, teachers sent by the Freedmen's Bureau to educate ex-slaves were housed here. The house was built in 1835 with slave labor. It is rumored there is a tunnel from its basement to the corner of Beale and Danny Thomas Boulevard, built to aid runaway slaves. The ghost of Uncle Nathan, a slave who buried the Hunt family silver to protect it from theft by Union troops, reportedly makes his presence known from time to time.

The home was finally restored to its owner, Colonel Hunt, by order of President Andrew Johnson, but Federal troops had stripped it bare. The Phelans, related to the Hunts by marriage, still own the house, and Stephen Rice Phelan is the fifth generation of his family to live there.

Courtesy of Memphis Room, MASPLIC

Sherman and his officers in Memphis. Sherman had command of Memphis from July 21 to December 20, 1862. He was replaced by General S. A. Hurlbut.

From The Photographic History of the Civil War

The Overton Hotel at the northwest corner of Main and Poplar at the site of Ellis Auditorium. The hotel was built in 1859, was used as a hospital during the Civil War, then as a hotel, and from 1873 until 1909 it was the Shelby County Court House. The inset shows a touched up photograph depicting a proposed expansion of the building, probably toward the end of the nineteenth century. It never took place. A new court house was built in 1909.

Courtesy of Memphis Transit Authority

Memphis' first steam fire engine, ordered in 1861, wasn't delivered until 1863, because of a Union blockade. It was brought out for this picture in the 1890s at the Front Street station.

Courtesy of Memphis Fire Department

Memphian W. F. Taylor served in the Seventh Tennessee Cavalry and attained the rank of lieutenant colonel. Confederate leaders after the war were in a precarious position. Military Governor Andrew Johnson suggested at one time that those who wouldn't sign a loyalty oath should be executed. He felt the leaders should suffer. For four years of reconstruction, ex-Confederates were denied the vote. Disloyal newspapers were closed and clergymen who preached sedition were imprisoned. W.F. Taylor, like others who served with him, had the respect of the people of Memphis, and he returned to the city to become a leading cotton factor and president of several companies. Many ex-Confederates, after losing everything, built a second fortune after the war.

Courtesy of Scott Rightor Jacobs

A tintype of a Memphis woman in the 1860s. A modification of the ambrotype, the procedure required a thin metal plate japanned black or brown as support for the light-sensitive collodion emulsion. The materials were cheaper than those needed for the daguerreotype. The photographer could obtain several images on one sheet of metal with a multilens camera, and then, after processing, cut them into single pictures with tin snips.

Courtesy of Catharine Richey Hinton

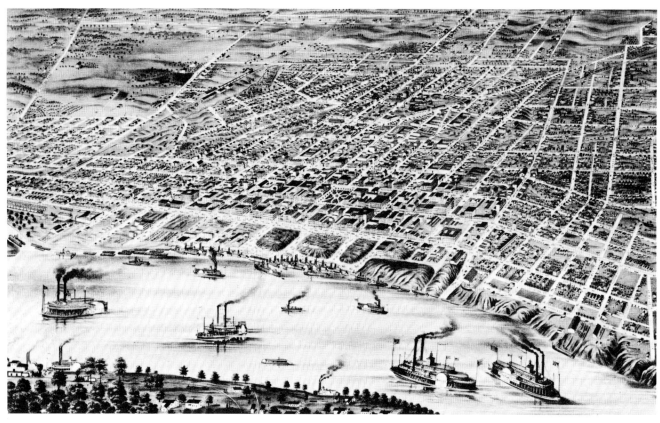

A bird's eye view of Memphis in 1870.

Courtesy of Charles Aste, Jr.

The Cole Manufacturing Co. dates back to 1866,
when it began selling lumber, glass, paint, and oil.
This photograph was taken in 1877, and shows the
manufacturing operations on Fourth Street.

Courtesy of Cole Manufacturing Co.

1865-1880

These years are characterized by strife. Most Tennesseans objected to Yankee rule and radical exploitation of the black vote. The Ku Klux Klan was organized and Governor Brownlow sought to punish ex-Confederates. Tense race relations in Memphis exploded in a riot in 1866, in which forty-four blacks were killed and their schools and churches burned. But by 1870, Memphis was recovered from the war. There were five daily newspapers, three suburbs. With a population of forty thousand and growing, the city seemed on the verge of prosperity.

Then yellow fever struck four times, beginning in 1867 and climaxing in 1878 and 1879. In all, over ten thousand people died. Many left for a more healthful clime. Some waited out the epidemics, then returned; others met opportunity elsewhere or lost faith and never returned.

The poor stayed, or joined camps established outside the city. All business ceased other than the business of tending the sick and burying the dead. The Howard Association, the Catholic Church and Citizens' Relief Committee, and two military companies composed of blacks were credited with preserving order and running the hospitals.

In the end, the city's debt was so high and recovery seemed so distant, Memphis' charter was repealed and the area became merely a taxing district. Its population, which had doubled between 1860 and 1870, declined in the decade of the fever and stood at 33,592, in 1880.

Apparently no photographic record of the fever exists. If photographs were taken, they were likely burned along with the belongings of the stricken or scattered by looters. Who knows? But the fever's impact altered the face and character of Memphis and delayed its prosperity by many years.

Many yellow fever victims were buried in Elmwood Cemetery, as were the founders of Memphis, who were moved from Winchester and Morris cemeteries as the city grew. Over two thousand Confederate dead are buried here. And in an unmarked grave lies Annie Cook, a madam who turned her house of shame on Gayoso Street into a hospital to nurse the fever victims. She, also, soon died of yellow fever. The cemetery, on South Dudley, dates from the 1850s. This photograph was taken around 1900.

Courtesy of Memphis Room, MASPLIC

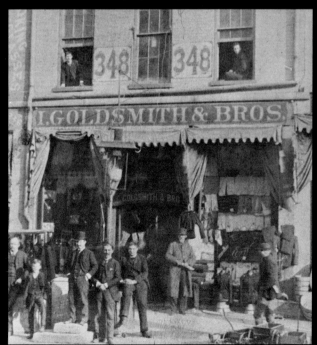

In 1870, Isaac and Jacob Goldsmith opened a dry goods store on Beale Street between Front and Main. In this picture, they posed in front of I. Goldsmith & Bros. In 1881, they moved their store to Main at Union, then in 1896 to a five-story building at Main and Gayoso.

Courtesy of Goldsmith's

The Fontaine House on Adams, built in 1870-71, was bought by Noland Fontaine, a cotton factor, in 1883. While the Fontaines resided there, it was the setting of elaborate parties, and its guests included John Philip Sousa and the son of Abraham Lincoln. Deeded to the city for use by the Memphis Art Association along with the Lee House, it was restored by the Memphis Chapter of the Association for the Preservation of Tennessee Antiquities with financial help from the State of Tennessee, the City of Memphis, Shelby County, and the State Association for the Preservation of Tennessee Antiquities. It was opened to the public in 1961.

Courtesy of Memphis Housing Authority

The Beale Street Baptist Church, built in 1869, was once the largest black church in the South. This photo was taken in the 1970s.

Courtesy of Memphis Room, MASPLIC

Noland and Virginia Eanes Fontaine about 1870. These daguerreotypes were encased in decorative gold and velvet.

Courtesy of Dr. Roland Bill

This house was built by Colonel William F. Taylor on Poplar Street in the late 1860s. It stood next to the Four Flames Restaurant until it was torn down in 1961.

Courtesy of Scott Rightor Jacobs

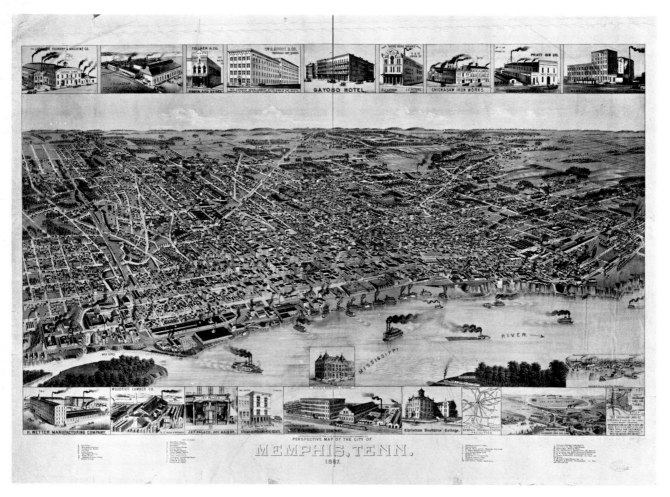

Perspective map of Memphis, 1887. In the lower right hand corner is Hopefield, Arkansas, the point of connection for the railroad. In this picture, the railroad transfer *General Pierson* carries train cars across the river. Five years later the railroad bridge was built.

Courtesy of Charles Aste, Jr.

1880-1900

In the 1880s, everyone started taking pictures. Many varieties of hand cameras appeared on the market, but the most famous was invented by George Eastman in New York in 1888. He called it the Kodak. The whole camera had to be sent to the factory for developing. Soon he had improved it so that amateurs could do the processing as well.

In Memphis, a photographer named Coovert started recording the many stages in the processing of cotton. Many of his pictures appear in this book. Memphis was an apt subject for the photographer, professional or amateur, for it was filled with life and progress.

A board of health was established, a sewerage system instituted, the roads were paved. Memphis had its first garbage service, and discovered an artesian water supply. The fever was quarantined and its spread halted every time it threatened. New railroads entered the city and began to replace steamboats as the prime movers of the cotton crop.

The cotton industry had changed. The planters, with no money after the war, were forced to live and plant on credit, and the factors, in control of the money, gained control of production. Memphis became the largest inland cotton and hardwood lumber market in the world. In the wholesale grocery business, Memphis was fifth in the United States.

English cotton buyers introduced Memphis to the game of tennis. Great houses were built. Memphis gave land on the riverfront for a post office, a library, and a fire station. It repaid the municipal debt left over from the fever days and regained its charter. The first telephone call was made, and the first bridge across the Mississippi south of St. Louis was built. The city's area quadrupled and, with the advent of steel foundations, the first downtown skyscraper was erected.

The dream of prosperity quelled by the yellow fever devastation of the 1870s had been realized, and the Bluff City's promise fulfilled. By 1900, Memphis was the third largest city in the South. Population exceeded one hundred thousand.

KING COTTON 'Long Live The King'
Member Central Agricultural Finance Corporation

On a plantation in Wilson, Arkansas, cotton was handpicked through the 1920s. The picker grabbed hold of the locks of the boll and yanked it out of the burr. At first baskets and flat cloths were used to hold the cotton. Later, pickers hung nine-foot cloth sacks over their shoulders by straps and dragged them along. Filled, the bags weighed a hundred pounds. Wilson, upriver in Mississippi County, probably shipped its cotton to Memphis by flatboat originally. Inland cotton growers loaded their crop on wagons pulled by ox teams and later shipped by rail.

Courtesy of Bert Odessa Wade

Showboats on the Mississippi in the first half of the century were small and family-operated. They got bigger and better, too big in fact to stop at the plantation communities, the little towns where they were most loved. Some had live animals, others gave medicine shows. The grandest ones arrived after their popularity began to decline. In 1900 there were about forty boats on Western rivers. By 1926, their number had dwindled to fourteen.

Courtesy of Bert Odessa Wade

Cotton was weighed in the 1890s on a scale similar to one still in use in 1931.

Courtesy of Memphis Room, MASPLIC

An early cotton gin. The slanted platform made it easy to roll the bales down onto drays.

Courtesy of Memphis Pink Palace Museum

Wagons waiting at the cotton gin. Each wagon held about one bale. After the inauguration of harvest machines and trailers, seven bales could be carried at one time.

Courtesy of Memphis Room, MASPLIC

This man was photographed carrying a bundle of cotton samples in the office of Godfrey Frank & Co.

Courtesy of Henry Frank

Abe H. Frank and John S. Williams examine cotton samples in the 1890s. The cotton buyers judged cotton by pulling and twisting a small piece to determine the length of the fibers.

Courtesy of Henry Frank

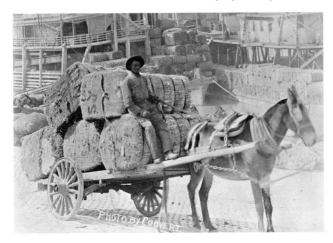

Open-sided drays loaded with cotton bales were pulled by mules from Front Row to the river. Here, a Lee Line steamer and the *J. N. Harbin* wait for a load. In 1913, the first cotton bales were transported by automobile.

Courtesy of Bert Odessa Wade

In 1867 Henry Montgomery built the first cotton compress in Memphis. This compress, in a warehouse, was being used to remake substandard bales. The one in the picture appears to be undersized. In 1896 the Cotton Exchange advocated the adoption of standard sized bales, twenty-eight inches wide by fifty-four inches long. Each one weighed 480 pounds.

Courtesy of Memphis Room, MASPLIC

At a warehouse at Virginia and Mississippi Avenues,
an elaborate method of moving the bales from the
gin to the loading dock and warehouses was in use in
the 1890s. In this early method of warehouse
mechanization, a mule could move thousands of
pounds.

Courtesy of Memphis Room, MASPLIC

The Cotton Exchange was established in 1873 for the promotion of cotton interests in Memphis. The organization improved telegraph facilities, issued crop reports, improved railroad handling, and decided on a standard size for bales. Millions of dollars worth of cotton were bought and sold with a handshake the only contract. This building, on Second between Court and Madison, was built to house the exchange in 1885.

Courtesy of Memphis Room, MASPLIC

Telegraph facilities allowed the exchange to have Memphis cotton on the major world markets. In this picture, Abe Frank gets a reading from Liverpool in the 1890s.

Courtesy of Henry Frank

Most cotton business was conducted on Front Row, where brokers, buyers, classers, weighers, compress hands, and clerks all participated in the moving of the crop. This picture, looking north, was taken in the 1890s.

Courtesy of Henry Frank

In 1931, the United States crop estimate of over
eleven million bales was posted. Memphis handled a
third of the total.

Courtesy of Memphis Room, MASPLIC

People lined the top of the bank as steamboats arrived in the 1890s. The building to the right of the library housed Otto Schwill & Co. and the Cummins Grocery Co. Paducah Coal supplied steamboats from its small building at the foot of Cossitt Library.

Courtesy of Memphis Room, MASPLIC

A riverfront scene, late 1890s. The Bohlen-Huse Ice Co. wagon is in the background.

Courtesy of Memphis Room, MASPLIC

The Kate Adams, the *J. N. Harbin,* and the *Ferd Herold* lined the riverfront in 1910. The inset shows the *Kate Adams* underway. It was the third "Lovin' Kate." The first, built in 1882, was named for the wife of Major John D. Adams of Little Rock, the owner of the Memphis & Arkansas City Packet Co. All three burned. Fire destroyed this one at the Memphis wharf in 1927.The first mail was carried by steamboat by Henry Shreve's *Post Boy* in 1819.

Courtesy of Bert Odessa Wade

The Lee Line

Steamboating was born about the same time as Jim Lee. And a true sibling he was, for he, too, belonged on the river. By the time he located in Memphis, in 1856, he had already spent over half his forty-eight years on steamboats. He soon owned his own line of boats when most other lines were owned by corporations. He was one of the best loved of the riverboat captains, known for his stories of boiler explosions and harrowing races, and his mammoth size. A special chair had to be built to contain him. When he died in 1889, every steamboat that approached Memphis for thirty days lowered its flag to half mast. His sons, Stacker and James, Jr., continued the line and James, Jr.'s son Robert E. at one time had fourteen boats steaming on the Mississippi, most bearing family names, as each of James, Jr.'s ten children had a steamer named for him or her. After 1910, the boats began losing money, but Captain G. Peters Lee continued on until the last boat, the *Harry Lee,* was sold in 1931 and remodeled for the excursion trade. Rosa Lee, a granddaughter of Jim Lee, deeded the Lee and Fontaine houses to the city for the James Lee Memorial Academy of Arts.

The *Georgia Lee,* built in the 1890s, had silver doorknobs and luxurious furnishings. She was called "Silk Stockings Georgia."

Courtesy of Dr. Roland Bill

An early Lee Line steamer, the *Robert E. Lee,* shared its illustrious name with many Mississippi riverboats. John W. Cannon's *Rob't E. Lee* beat the Natchez in the famous race from New Orleans to St. Louis in 1870 and was already winning by an hour and two minutes at Memphis. Top speed on steamboats was about twenty-five miles per hour.

Courtesy of Bert Odessa Wade

This picture shows the variety of goods shipped by steamboat. Although cotton was always the most important passenger, such diverse things as furniture and wine were shipped from Memphis even before the Civil War.

Courtesy of Frank Garavelli

By the 1930s, the levee has become a parking lot and the *U. S. Willow* waits, but not for cotton.

Courtesy of Memphis Pink Palace Museum

The United States Snag Boat *Macomb,* about 1890. Snags on the river bottom, the principal cause of steamboat accidents, were a fact of life until 1827, when the War Department appointed Henry Shreve to the task of river improvement. He had invented the snag boat, a vessel with twin hulls. It wedged snags into an iron-plated jaw, yanked them from the river bottom, then sawed them into small, harmless pieces and dumped them out the back. It worked so well that five years later no snag accidents were reported for a whole year.

Courtesy of Bert Odessa Wade

Gambling on a boat around 1900.

Courtesy of Robert Ledbetter

By the 1930s, many of the old steamers like the
Idlewild had been turned over to the excursion trade.

Courtesy of Robert Ledbetter

A formal dining area of an early twentieth century
riverboat. Many of the boats were luxurious, with
linen and monogrammed silver, china specially designed,
ceilings of polished cherry, imported Brussels carpets,
and delicate crystal chandeliers. The typical menu
might have included turtle soup, baked fish, turkey
with oyster sauce, stuffed crabs, artichokes, pastries,
and fruit.

Courtesy of Robert Ledbetter

The hardwood industry rivaled wholesale groceries and cotton for the place of economic honor. In this picture, a mule-drawn flatcar transports a sawmill owner's family, friends, and dog into the forest in 1900 to watch the wood cutting. Lumber railroads were used beginning in the 1880s.

Courtesy of Bert Odessa Wade

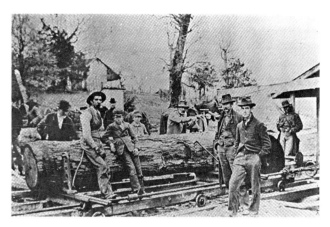

This sawmill was located on West Street in Germantown in the 1890s.

Courtesy of Harry Cloyes

The Yazoo & Mississippi Valley, with two engines in the lead, carries lumber to market. By 1893, engines had been designed to exceed speeds of one hundred miles per hour.

Courtesy of Memphis Room, MASPLIC

The Yazoo and Mississippi Valley Depot, Calhoun and Main, April 17, 1894. The building was torn down in 1912 to make way for the new Central Station.

Courtesy of Memphis Room, MASPLIC

The Illinois Central Depot, at Poplar and Front Streets. In the 1880s, seven new rail lines came to Memphis. In the 1890s, the Illinois Central purchased the Chesapeake, Ohio & Southwestern, and the Louisville, New Orleans & Texas and consolidated them into a single system.

Courtesy of Memphis Room, MASPLIC

The first Mississippi bridge at Memphis, built by the Kansas City Fort Scott and Memphis Railroad, opened May 12, 1892. A crowd of fifty thousand went to the opening to watch the eighteen locomotives chug across. Then, it was the third longest bridge in the world, and the only one south of St. Louis on the Mississippi. The engineers and firemen who volunteered for the first crossing were lauded for their bravery. In 1903, it was sold to the Frisco railroad and became the Frisco Bridge. Most road traffic still went by ferry, though wagons and carriages could cross it on planks laid between the rails.

Courtesy of Robert Ledbetter

Men of the Illinois Central around 1900.

Courtesy of Audrey and Harry Osborn

The railroads were both a boon and a forewarning of doom to the steamboat era. They helped by speeding cotton to the river, then their efficiency and speed by comparison made the boats almost seem superfluous. Here, around 1900, a boy wearing a Gayoso Co. cap has a good view of both.

Courtesy of Memphis Pink Palace Museum

This Illinois Central engine was eleventh in a line of eighteen engines coupled together to make the test run on the first Memphis Bridge, later called Frisco Bridge, May 12, 1892. Left to right are J. J. Schmidt, Frank Schmidt, S. A. Law, and Bill Worden.

Courtesy of Memphis Room, MASPLIC

Victorian clutter characterizes this Memphis woman's room. In the 1890s, filling every inch of space was the fashion, and decorators advised leaving only space enough to move around.

In 1886, these boys were dressed for a Conway School graduation. The photo is by Gebhardt, an early Memphis photographer.

Courtesy of Scott Rightor Jacobs

Fifty-two students of the Christian Brothers in Memphis attended the World Industrial and Cotton Centennial Exposition in New Orleans in 1885 and were photographed on the *Liberty Bell.*

Courtesy of Christian Brothers College

Shelby County Poor and Insane Asylum, built before 1900, was located six miles northeast of the city on Old Raleigh Road.

Courtesy of Memphis Room, MASPLIC

Memphis High School, on Poplar near Danny Thomas Boulevard, about 1900. Until 1911, it was the only white public high school in Memphis. Public education had begun in March of 1848, due to the efforts of G. B. Locke, J. W. A. Pettit, and Eugene Magevney. The first buildings specifically for schools were not erected until after the war. In 1886, the first building tax was levied.

Courtesy of Bert Odessa Wade

Money for the Cossitt Library building was given to the city by the children of Frederick Henry Cossitt, who had made his fortune in Memphis before the Civil War. The city donated land intended in the original plat as public promenade, and the red sandstone building overlooking the river was completed in 1893. The newspapers and the Nineteenth Century Club sponsored book campaigns, and General Colton Greene and J. M. Keating donated their private libraries, and other Memphians made large contributions. A new building on the site was erected in 1950.

Courtesy of Robert Ledbetter

This house was built by Robertson Topp on the southeast corner of Beale and Lauderdale. In the late 1870s or early 1880s, Miss Jenny Higbee bought it for her girls' school. Until it closed in 1914, the school was the fashionable place for young Memphis girls to get an education.

Courtesy of Memphis Room, MASPLIC

The steps of the Cossitt Library, with their view of the levee, were a favorite spot for picture taking, or just watching the boats being loaded with cotton. This picture was taken about 1910.

Courtesy of Mrs. Oscar F. Blomberg

The Cossitt Library Museum in the early 1900s.

Courtesy of Memphis Room, MASPLIC

Mrs. Johnson's story hour at the library in the 1920s.

Courtesy of Memphis Room, MASPLIC

The Nineteenth Century Club was organized in 1890 with thirty members for the purpose of providing a reading room and intellectual center for Memphis women. Their first meeting place was a single room in the Collier Building. In 1892, they secured a charter from the state. This building, on Union, was bought by the club in the 1920s. In 1909 in Memphis there were over thirty women's clubs, including the Women's Club, a literary organization founded in 1890, the Talkitanti Club, founded by Mrs. Gilbert D. Raine, and the Salon Circle, organized by Memphis Jewish women in 1903. Nationally, by 1910, almost a million ladies belonged to clubs, and their accomplishments included enlightened child labor laws, a juvenile court system, and support of charitable institutions.

Courtesy of Bert Odessa Wade

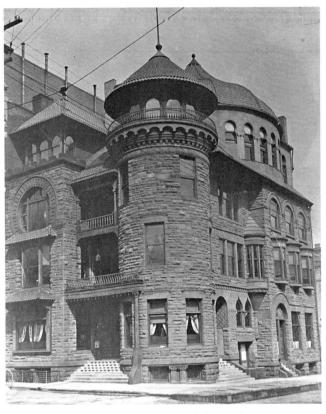

This building, at North Court and Second, was erected in 1895 to house the Tennessee Club. The club, founded in 1875 by General Colton Greene, is one of the oldest Southern social groups in existence. Construction cost forty-four thousand dollars. The building has a round dining room and ballroom and a view of Court Square. By the 1970s, the Tennessee Club had moved to the top floor of the 100 North Main Building and the law firm of Burch, Porter and Johnson had offices in their old quarters.

Courtesy of Bert Odessa Wade

The William Roland Harris home on Central Avenue. William Harris, a Tennessee Supreme Court Justice, was the brother of Isham G. Harris, the Democratic governor of Tennessee from 1857 through the Civil War. Isham Harris resided in the home when Nashville fell. He had favored secession and to escape arrest after the war ended, he fled to Mexico where he joined other Confederates to found a new South. From there he went to England, then returned to Tennessee in 1867, after the five thousand dollar reward for his capture had been repealed. He was elected to the United States Senate in 1877 and controlled the state sovereignty faction of Tennessee Democrats until his death in 1897. The home was bought in 1953 by Mrs. Edward Otto Schwamm for her daughters Lois Claire and Ann Sawyer Schwamm. They maintain a formal boxwood garden at the spot on its lawn where Nathan Bedford Forrest's men rendezvoused to plan raids into Mississippi. When the home was built, in 1853, its grounds covered forty acres. Now there are three and a half.

Courtesy of Bert Odessa Wade

The Joseph Newberger home at the southeast corner of Union and Parkway. In the early 1920s, Joseph Newberger, president of the Newberger Cotton Co., bought the whole balcony of the auditorium for a performance and gave the tickets away to promote opera in Memphis. In the 1970s, the house was occupied by Memphis Theological Seminary.

Courtesy of Bert Odessa Wade

The Montgomery home, which stood on the northeast corner of Poplar and Montgomery, at the site of Memphis Technical High School, was built in the late 1860s or early 1870s by Henry A. Montgomery. He had come to Memphis in 1850 from his native Ireland. He was twenty-three and poor and began as a laborer rolling cotton. By 1860 he owned a telegraph service and had laid the first telegraph cable across the Mississippi River at Memphis. After the war, he built a large cotton compress and became one of the wealthiest men in the city. His home was the site of many lavish parties, including a reception in 1882 for Oscar Wilde, who had lectured to six hundred Memphians at Lubrie's Theatre. Eighteen-eighty-two also marked the beginning of horse racing in Memphis, with the opening of Montgomery Park, named for Henry A. Montgomery, its founder.

Courtesy of Bert Odessa Wade

The Gilbert D. Raine home was built of castellated stone at the corner of Union and McNeil in the 1890s. Gilbert Raine arrived in Memphis from Virginia in 1870, finished his education at the high schools and became a clerk for the Hernando Insurance Co. Later, he became a representative of several well-known national insurance companies and at one time was doing the largest insurance business in the South. In 1889, he formed with W. J. Crawford, John Overton, Jr., and W. B. Mallory, the Democrat Publishing Co. and the first issue of a new paper, *The Memphis Daily Commercial,* appeared that December. In 1894 *The Memphis Appeal, The Avalanche* and *The Memphis Daily Commercial* were consolidated to form *The Commercial Appeal.*

Courtesy of Bert Odessa Wade

The home of John Overton, Jr., a descendant of one of Memphis' founders. It stood at Bellevue and Union, the site, since 1918, of Methodist Hospital.

Courtesy of Bert Odessa Wade

The French Renaissance house of Napoleon Hill, built at a cost of forty-five thousand dollars in the late 1870s, stood at the corner of Third and Madison until it was torn down and the Sterick Building erected on the site in 1929. It had huge stables at the rear. In 1850, when Napoleon Hill was twenty, news arrived that gold had been found at Sutter's Mill. He quit his job as a store clerk in Bolivar, Tennessee, and joined a wagon train as an outrider. He never found much gold, but started a grocery and liquor store for the miners that served him just as well. With his profit, he set up a supply business in Memphis and became wealthy, providing stores for the planters. He was later president of the Chamber of Commerce and Cotton Exchange and a founder of Union Planters Bank. At one time he owned a large portion of downtown Memphis. His wife was a president of the Beethoven Club, founded in 1888 to promote culture in Memphis.

Courtesy of Bert Odessa Wade

The William Ball home at the site of Methodist Hospital, Bellevue and Union. This photograph was taken about 1910. The house was built before the turn of the century.

Courtesy of Bert Odessa Wade

The Mallory home was built in the 1890s at a cost of forty-five thousand dollars, by Captain W. B. Mallory. It is at the site of the Lamar Unit of Baptist Hospital. Captain Mallory, a Confederate veteran from North Carolina, moved to Memphis in 1869 and engaged in the insurance business. He later was a partner in the company Mallory, Crawford & Co., wholesale grocers, cotton factors, and commission merchants.

Courtesy of Bert Odessa Wade

The Miller home, in 1916, probably the residence of William E. Miller of Germantown. Miller farmed and owned a pharmacy there and was postmaster from 1872 to 1878. His son, also William E. Miller, attended Leddin's Business College in Memphis, then continued the drug business in Germantown.

Courtesy of Ray Fizer

On the north side of Union between Bellevue and Claybrook stood the Watkins Overton home. Watkins Overton was elected to the Tennessee State Legislature in 1925, the Senate in 1927, and was mayor of Memphis from 1928 to 1940 and from 1948 to 1952. The home was torn down in 1918. The back of the John Overton home may be seen to the left in this photograph.

Courtesy of Bert Odessa Wade

Dr. Heber Jones enters his carriage on Adams Avenue, between Manassas and Orleans. After graduating from medical school in Virginia, he studied abroad, then came to Memphis to practice in 1872. He served as president of the board of health beginning in 1878 and was a member of the State Board of Medical Examiners.

Courtesy of Henry Frank

The Marks home on Adams, between Manassas and Orleans, 1890s.

Courtesy of Henry Frank

The home of Frank G. Jones, formerly on Vance, in the 1890s. Jones was vice president of the Memphis Street Railway Co. and people liked to call him "Streetcar Jones." He followed the race horse circuit and entertained nationally prominent people in this home that in later years had several additions. The house in the 1970s was occupied by Southern Funeral Home. Parked in front is Jones' horseless carriage, one of the first in Memphis.

Courtesy of Bert Odessa Wade

The D. T. Porter French Renaissance home stood on the southeast corner of Vance and Orleans. Porter was born in Robertson County, Tennessee, in 1827, came to Memphis in 1857. The former druggist became a grocer and commission merchant and served as president of the Memphis Taxing District. His family, as a memorial, bought the multi-story structure known as the D. T. Porter Building.

Courtesy of Bert Odessa Wade

The Carnes home at Linden and Wellington, built before the turn of the century. General S. T. Carnes introduced the first telephone to Memphis and the first electric light, and he owned one of the first automobiles. He became president and general manager of the Memphis Electric Light and Power Co., commanded the Tennessee militia, and served as captain of the Chickasaw Guards.

Courtesy of Memphis Room, MASPLIC

The Elias Lowenstein home, at the northwest corner of Jefferson and Manassas. The building has been enlarged on the west side. The Lowensteins first engaged in the wholesale of dry goods in Memphis in 1861, when Benedict Lowenstein opened B. Lowenstein and Brothers on Main Street.

Courtesy of Henry Frank

One of Memphis' best loved and most colorful leaders, David Park Hadden, a Kentuckian, came to Memphis in 1870. He prospered in the cotton business and helped found the Memphis Mardi Gras. He was chosen president of the Memphis Taxing District when Memphis surrendered its charter in January 1879, and was largely responsible for cleaning up the city and restoring public morale. Later, "Pappy" Hadden was police court judge and opened each court session with the words, "The show is on." So many of the stabbings that were tried by his court were caused by crooked gambling, he invented a dice rolling contraption to assure a fair roll. It was called the Hadden Horn. This photograph was taken around 1890.

Courtesy of Memphis Pink Palace Museum

David Park Hadden on a mule at Pike's Peak in 1886. The mule was his usual mode of transportation, even in Memphis, where he rode a mule named Hulda to town from his mansion on Rayburn. It wasn't until after the Civil War that Memphians, as well as other Americans, traveled long distances for pleasure. By the 1870s, though, the railroad had completed its transcontinental service, and people could afford to see other parts of the country.

Courtesy of Memphis Pink Palace Museum

The Fire Department had new headquarters erected in 1891 on Front at Union. The Cossitt Library is to the right in the photo.

Courtesy of Memphis Fire Department

This horse-drawn Babcock Aerial was purchased by the city in 1891 for 3,350 dollars. The ladder was eighty-five feet long, the chemical engine pumped sixty to eighty gallons. Fire engines were horse drawn until about 1918. In this picture the Babcock's ladder is demonstrated on a three-story building on Front Street.

Courtesy of Memphis Fire Department

A horse-drawn fire wagon in action, 1890s.

Courtesy of Memphis Pink Palace Museum

In the late 1890s, Mencken Department Store and the Gayoso Hotel burned. In this picture, an amateur photographer recorded the first billow of smoke as it invaded Front Street.

Courtesy of Mrs. Oscar F. Blomberg

A bike rider on a downtown Memphis street around 1900. In the 1890s Memphis had a bike racing track west of East End Park. Then, bicycles were called "wheels."

Courtesy of Henry Frank

Looking east on Madison Avenue in the 1890s, and in 1941. Both photographs were taken from the Post Office steps.

Courtesy of Memphis Room, MASPLIC

South Court Street in the 1890s. The S. C. Toof Co.,
at the end of the street on Second, dates from 1864.
In the 1890s it had become the largest printing
establishment in the South. To the right is the old
Gaston Hotel, begun in 1867 by the Frenchman John
Gaston, who came to Memphis after the war as a
wounded, penniless Confederate private. After a life of
wandering and learning the business of chef from
Paris to California to Delmonico's in New York, he
settled in Memphis, where he remained, even through
the yellow fever years. He bought all the property he
could and by the turn of the century was extremely
wealthy. He gave to Memphis the Gaston Community
Center and the John Gaston Hospital.

Courtesy of Memphis Room, MASPLIC

Collier, Hall & Co., feed sale and commission stables, was located on Union in the 1890s. The sale of mules and horses was a two and a third million dollars a year business in Memphis in 1899. In August and September, trainloads of cattle arrived from Texas, Oklahoma, Colorado, and the West. Mules came from Missouri, Kansas, and Illinois, and blooded horses from Kentucky, Indiana, Illinois, and Ohio. All converged near the corner of Third and Monroe Streets, the stock district of Memphis, and from October to May business was brisk. One year in the 1940s, over seventy-five thousand mules were sold for over ten million dollars.

Courtesy of Memphis Room, MASPLIC

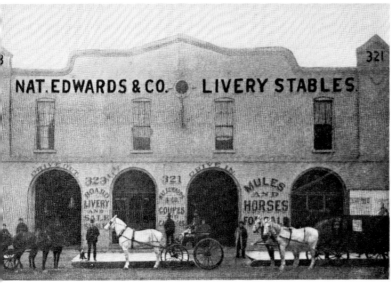

Nat Edward & Co. Livery, Sale and Boarding Stables, formerly were located on Second Street. In 1899, the average mule sold for ninety dollars, the average horse for fifty dollars.

Courtesy of Memphis Room, MASPLIC

The Lockwood Stable, at Third and Monroe, 1899.

Courtesy of Memphis Room, MASPLIC

Looking north on Main Street, 1895.

Courtesy of Memphis Room, MASPLIC

Berton's Confectionery moved from Poplar and
Fourth to Beale in 1877. Here, the proprietors, Mr.
and Mrs. Frank Bensieck, pose with their employees
at the new location. In 1868, Berton's had become the
first place in Memphis to serve ice cream every day,
and they even had a secluded separate parlor for
unescorted ladies.

Courtesy of Charles Aste, Jr.

A. Schwab celebrated one hundred years on Beale
Street in 1976. This picture was made at a sale in the
1890s. The family-owned dry goods store had become
a partial museum in the 1970s, Mr. Schwab having
collected memorabilia as the street changed around
him.

Courtesy of A. Schwab

The Tennessee Brewing Co. principals gathered for this advertisement extolling the merits of Tennessee Lager Beer in the 1890s. The 1891 Souvenir Edition of the *Memphis Evening Scimitar* carried a picture of the plant on its cover, and praised its president, John W. Schorr, for his fine quality beer.

Courtesy of Robert Ledbetter

The Tennessee Brewery, on the southwest corner of
Butler and Tennessee Streets, in the late 1890s. Then,
it was the largest brewery in the South. In 1954 it was
bought by A. Karchmer & Son Metals. The scrap
metal recycling business still occupied the ground
floor in the seventies, and pigeons had taken over the
upper stories.

Courtesy of Memphis Room, MASPLIC

The Clarendon Hotel, on the south side of Madison
near Third Street, in 1895.

Courtesy of Memphis Transit Authority

The Chickasaw Guards group was formed as a citizens' protective organization in 1874 with sixty-five members. Under their first captain, R. P. Duncan, they ordered fifty dollar blue uniforms from New York. The state of Tennessee equipped them with fifty-caliber Springfield rifles. They were the first uniformed Tennessee military company since the war. Prior to the Civil War, the Rifle Guards, the George Washington Riflemen, the Washington Rifle Company, the Steuben Artillery, and countless other groups drilled in Memphis. By 1900, the number of military organizations was smaller, and the companies were more exclusive. This caricature, significance unknown, was taken by Bingham Brothers Photographers, probably in the 1890s.

Courtesy of Memphis Pink Palace Museum

The Second Infantry Regiment of the Tennessee National Guard, photographed around the turn of the century.

Courtesy of Mississippi Valley Collection
Memphis State University Libraries

President Benjamin Harrison's reception in Memphis
in 1891. He lost re-election the next year to Cleveland.

Courtesy of Memphis Room, MASPLIC

Raleigh was popular as a health resort as early as 1842. Hotels were built and doctors prescribed its rest and waters for the cure of many ills. Raleigh spring water was bottled and sold in Memphis drug stores. The tobacco millionaire B. I. Duke built the Raleigh Springs Inn, shown in this photograph in the 1890s, and it was a popular vacation spot for Memphians until around 1910. It became a sanitarium and a few years later burned.

Courtesy of Memphis Room, MASPLIC

In 1892, a streetcar line opened between Memphis and Raleigh.

Courtesy of Memphis Room, MASPLIC

A group of Memphians on the steps of the Raleigh
Springs Inn, about 1903.

Courtesy of Henry Frank

In 1886, the Louisville, New Orleans & Texas Railroad owned one million acres of land along the southern part of its route and wanted to settle it with blacks because it was thought that whites couldn't survive the climate. They approached I. T. Montgomery, a former slave of Joseph Davis, Jefferson Davis' brother, who was educated and owned a large plantation. Montgomery founded the all-Negro town of Mound Bayou and came to Memphis in July to recruit new citizens for it. This photograph of Montgomery and five of his six daughters was taken in 1888.

Courtesy of Dr. Roland Bill

Swimmers jumped from the Wolf River bridge at Raleigh in the first decade of the twentieth century. The river, one hundred miles in length, once carried river boats to Germantown and Bolivar. In the 1800s, farmers could float their crops from branches into the Wolf and on to market at Memphis. It was also the main source of drinking water until an artesian supply was discovered in 1887.

Courtesy of Memphis Pink Palace Museum

A scene at Raleigh Springs, about 1900.

Courtesy of Memphis Public Library

This baby enjoyed the attentions of mother,
grandmother, and nurse, in 1902.

Courtesy of Catharine Richey Hinton

Bible reading, probably in the 1890s.

Courtesy of Memphis Room, MASPLIC

A baptism during high water on the Lewis Bayou, about 1900. In 1891, blacks supported twenty-three Baptist and ten Methodist churches in Memphis.

Courtesy of Dr. Roland Bill

An arch of cotton was a sure sign of an imminent
parade. This one was photographed on Second Street,
about 1900.

Courtesy of Mississippi Valley Collection
Memphis State University Libraries

1900-1920

Looking back, the early 1900s seem like one continuous parade. Memphians regaled heroes and presidents and Confederate veterans, and ushered in Mayor Crump with parades. They paraded for women's rights and civic pride and support of the Allies. Lacking a special occasion, they paraded anyway, to show off that new invention, the automobile, or a new race horse.

In 1910, there were a mere thousand automobiles in Memphis. Three years later there were over six thousand. The first speed limit was set at eight miles per hour and no doubt the first speeder promptly broke it.

Horse racing flourished with a new driving park, then quickly died after betting was outlawed. Vaudeville reached its peak, then gave way to nickelodeons and downtown movies.

The city established a park commission and Overton and Riverside and Confederate parks were developed, along with the city's first zoo. The Harahan Bridge, the second across the Mississippi at Memphis, was opened, and railroads were replacing steamboats as the major means of transport.

It was a time of reform. Tennessee became a dry state in 1909, and in 1913, Congress passed the Webb-Kenyon Act over Taft's veto, making it illegal to bring liquor in, and paving the way to national prohibition.

Memphis adopted a commission form of government. Edward Hull Crump began building his powerful political machine, and the Mississippi, with the help of a steamboat stuck in low water, built Mud Island. Other builders changed the city's skyline with the nineteen-story Exchange Building, and the twenty-story Commercial Trust & Savings Co. building. The city limits were extended and Binghampton, one of many small communities to meet the same fate, was annexed. By 1920, the population had grown to 162,351. Enterprising businessmen opened the first self-service grocery and the first five and dime, and busy criminals made Memphis number one in the nation in crime.

For a nickel, a kid could ride a streetcar or see a movie. Or if his pockets were empty, he could go down to the river and watch the boats steam in or marvel at the many new inventions, including the typewriter and the sewing machine.

Public opinion vehemently opposed the new trend of women entering business as "lady typewriters," and a *Commercial Appeal* editor stated he could see no practical use for another new invention, the airplane

These children display the fashion of the day: long woolen stockings and laced shoes for girls, the stiff collar and knickers for boys.

Courtesy of Mrs. Robert Haney

A parade heads north on Union at Main, about 1905.

Courtesy of Henry Frank

An unidentified parade through a black community, about 1920. The Mosaic Templars of America, the group in the draped vehicle, was one of many secret societies formed since emancipation.

*Courtesy of Mississippi Valley Collection
Memphis State University Libraries*

Basket lunches were a good reason for a church social
or other fundraising party. The men would bid on
baskets and get a lady to go with the lunch. Usually
they were held out-of-doors.

Courtesy of Henry Frank

A weekend house party in Ripley, Mississippi, about 1907. A Memphis photographer was asked along to record their fun.

Courtesy of Bert Odessa Wade

In 1907, five hundred, a variation of rummy, was a popular card game. Many young ladies decorated their own hats and wore them everywhere, even on a picnic.

Courtesy of Bert Odessa Wade

A family ride in the country.

Courtesy of Henry Frank

A family picnic in the early 1900s. Eight hundred acres of land were purchased by the Park Commission in 1900 to form Riverside and Overton parks. This picture could have been taken at Riverside, a popular picnic site in the early 1900s.

Courtesy of Henry Frank

In 1907 passengers boarded a summer car at Overton Park for five cents. The running board on the side folded down to form a step. The Jim Crow law, in effect since the summer of 1905, divided the car into separate sections for blacks and whites.

Courtesy of Bert Odessa Wade

A railroad car photographed about 1900. The cars were used by the railroad, by doctors, and by lumbermen, who needed to make unscheduled trips by rail. They were light enough to derail in the case of an oncoming train if no passing spur was in sight. This one was motor driven, but handcars were also used.

Courtesy of Audrey and Harry Osborn

The East End Park pavilion about 1900.

Courtesy of Memphis Room, MASPLIC

East End Park, on the north side of Madison, was served by the Dummy Line. In this photograph of the entrance, probably taken around 1910, all is quiet, but the Dummy Line was heavily traveled. There was a song about going "...on the Dummy didn't have no fare, Honey. They put me off at Idleware, Honey." Down the street at Madison and Cooper is the site of Overton Square.

Such vaudeville acts as Madame Irwin, the "Iron-Jawed Wonder of the Nineteenth Century," and the Ringling Brothers Circus, featuring "Speedy," who dove from seventy feet into a tub, came to East End Park through the early 1900s. Other attractions were the Orpheum Circuit in the open air theatre, a roller coaster, shooting galleries, dance bands, and refreshments. But movies were newer and when they invaded Main Street, East End crowds diminished. Prohibition in 1909 doomed the park to close. It was officially closed in 1913, and in March of 1924 its eight acres were sold and developed as a residential area. The building on the left was still standing in the 1970s.

Courtesy of Bert Odessa Wade

Vaudeville promised for ten cents to deliver the exotic, foreign, sensuous, and exciting. Troupes arrived by train or wagon and set up their tents in the most promising vacant lots. These pictures, all taken by Memphian Abe Frank around 1900, record the vaudeville attractions from the Lady who Flies Through the Air to the well-dressed ladies who were treated to camel rides. Eroticism was at times thinly veiled. On the Gay Paree sign to the right in the Flying Lady picture, prudish people are admonished to forego the entertainment.

Courtesy of Henry Frank

These musicians were photographed in a Memphis studio about 1910. In the early 1900s, bands proliferated. They were an important part of any political campaign, and were frequently hired to play for private parties in the large homes, on a bandstand in a park, or in Court Square. In 1909, the Croce Brothers String Band, Saxby's Military Band, and the Junior Confederate Memorial Drum and Fife Corps, were listed in the city directory for hire.

Courtesy of Audrey and Harry Osborn

Crowds turned out for vaudeville at Loew's State on the east side of Main between Gayoso and Beale. Ventriloquists, singers, jugglers, and animal acts were the usual fare. Double entendre songs and jokes began breaking down Victorian taboos.

Courtesy of Memphis Pink Palace Museum

The Majestic, on Main Street, charged ten cents for adults, five cents for children, and changed pictures daily.

Courtesy of Memphis Pink Palace Museum

The Overton Park Zoo traces its beginnings to 1901, when the Chicks baseball team donated their mascot to the city. Natch, a black bear, was tied to a tree in Overton Park. Others contributed a bobcat and raccoon. In 1903, the city built the first houses for the animals and hired a zookeeper. This picture of the Carnivora Building was taken about 1908.

Courtesy of Memphis Pink Palace Museum

The auditorium of the Goodwyn Institute at Second and Madison, at the site of First National Bank. The institute was willed to Tennessee by William A. Goodwyn in 1898 as a "great democratic educational institution." The building was erected in accordance with his will in 1907. It included rental offices, a 5,500-volume library and a nine-hundred-seat auditorium for free lectures. In the 1908-1909 season of programs, the Reverend Anna H. Shaw, a preacher and president of the National American Woman Suffrage Association, spoke on "The American Home." Jacob A. Riis of New York City, author, scholar, and lecturer, presented "Battle with the Slums," and Maude Ballington Booth lectured on "Lights and Shadows of Prison Life." In the 1950s, the building was traded with that of First National Bank, and First National erected new offices on the site. The lectures were moved to Memphis State University and the library holdings shelved in the Cossitt Library.

Courtesy of Bert Odessa Wade

This picture of Confederate Park was taken soon after it was laid out in 1908. The view is from the Custom House, and Front Street is on the right. The Civil War cannons, just visible on the left, were sacrificed during World War II when Washington called for scrap metal.

Courtesy of Memphis Pink Palace Museum

This is a view of Court Square in 1900. It was one of
four public squares originally in the city plan of 1819.
In 1826, a meeting house was built in the square
where Eugene Magevney taught school and where the
first ministers held church meetings. In the late 1850s,
a bust of Andrew Jackson was placed in the square
inscribed with the words, "Our union, it must be
preserved," from a toast he made as president.
Confederates took a chisel to the words at the time of
the Civil War. The city replaced them in 1908. The
statue was removed to the Court House in the early
1900s.

Courtesy of Robert Ledbetter

The Court Square Fountain, graced by a statue of
Hebe, cupbearer to the ancient Greek gods, was
installed in 1876, the gift of fifty Memphis citizens and
businesses.

Courtesy of Memphis Room, MASPLIC

J. V. Montedonico with his pacer Joe Lewis in Overton Park in 1909. Once an outfielder for the Chicks baseball team, he became president of State Savings, a bank his father founded.

Courtesy of Joseph V. Montedonico, Jr.

Mr. and Mrs. Arthur N. Seessel in a surrey at Overton Park, about 1910.

Courtesy of Arthur N. Seessel, Jr.

One of the first automobiles in Memphis, owned by
General Sam Carnes. With him are Mrs. Carnes, Miss
Juliet Carnes and Miss Nancy Martin. The auto
arrived in 1901.

Courtesy of Memphis Room, MASPLIC

Elias Lowenstein and his wife were photographed in a horseless carriage on Jefferson, around 1900.

Courtesy of Henry Frank

By about 1905, the automobile had begun to replace carriages for Sunday afternoon trips through Overton Park.

Courtesy of Mrs. Oscar F. Blomberg

With parasols to keep the sun off, these young women admired a friend's car around 1910.

Courtesy of Bert Odessa Wade

Miss Gill's eighth grade class at Dr. R.B. Maury
School in 1913.

Courtesy of Ray Fizer

In bow tie and overalls, the young man posed for this picture in front of Cumberland Presbyterian Church in the early 1900s. The Motley & Binney Electric Co. wagon featured a steam turbine powered electric fan. Ribbons were tied to the fan either to demonstrate its wind power or for safety.

Courtesy of Robert Ledbetter

The Shelby County Schools wagonette in 1915. In this picture, the driver had just picked up his charges from rural homes in Germantown. The first wagonettes were motorized in 1918, and by 1929 the county was converting trucks into buses. They were painted red, white, and blue, before law required that all school buses be yellow.

Courtesy of Harry Cloyes

Loeb's Laundry bought the first retail delivery truck in Memphis. In this picture, the fleet had expanded to five, one yet to be painted with the Loeb's logo. Henry Loeb opened his first laundry on Monroe in 1887. Deliveries were first made by two horse-drawn wagons.

Courtesy of Loeb's

The Arthur N. Seessel's Market delivery truck was a 1914 Model T Ford. They advertised six telephones to handle grocery orders.

Courtesy of Arthur N. Seessel, Jr.

The main office of Seessel's Market, about 1915.

Courtesy of Arthur N. Seessel, Jr.

The office of Dominic Canale. His secretary is taking
dictation that will be transcribed on one of the first
typewriters in Memphis. In 1870, there were only
seven female stenographers in America. By 1900, there
were over a hundred thousand.

Courtesy of John D. Canale

In 1910, the Standard Auto Supply Co.'s business
vehicle was an adapted towing car. The store, at the
corner of Second and Monroe, advertised Ajax tires,
guaranteed to last five thousand miles.

Courtesy of Memphis Pink Palace Museum

This downtown Memphis garage displayed new cars about 1910. The very small auto in the back center of the picture is a one-cylinder Reo. Despite its diminutive size, it could hold four people, counting the rumble seat, and attained a speed of thirty-five miles per hour. The car front right is a two-cylinder Reo and there are several more Reos, a Stoddard-Dayton, and a National in the picture.

Courtesy of Bert Odessa Wade

Justice of the Peace and Notary E. E. Strong shared offices with D. H. Pope and J. F. Brannon, both sheriff's deputies, on South Main Street in 1908. In the window is a poll tax notice.

Courtesy of Memphis Room, MASPLIC

Joe Spinoza's fruit wagon on Beale Street advertised Old Dominick Whiskey in 1907. Around 1900, no other brand exceeded its popularity in the mid-South. When prohibition came, D. Canale & Co., the distributor, diverted into other lines. Schenley Industries later bought the trademark for five thousand dollars to keep the popular name off the market.

Courtesy of John D. Canale

The fifteenth Mr. Bowers' Store, on Madison Avenue. Bowers came to Memphis in 1902 from Columbus, Kentucky, where he had suffered losses in the grocery business. In Memphis, with little capital, he opened a cut-rate store at Polk and McKinley and traded on a cash only basis. It was a different way of doing things, and it caught on. Duke C. Bowers owned thirty-seven stores by 1911. He was as well known for his generosity to the city in gifts of wading pools for children at Overton and Forrest parks, and other acts of charity.

Courtesy of Mississippi Valley Collection
Memphis State University Libraries

The interior of a Mr. Bowers' Store, about 1908.

Courtesy of Mississippi Valley Collection
Memphis State University Libraries

The Miller Paving Co., with offices at Beale and Orleans and also on Madison, advertised their concrete work at the construction site of a railroad bridge about 1909.

Courtesy of Audrey and Harry Osborn

In 1901, Goldsmith's expanded in a move across the street to its present downtown location. The store later expanded further to fill four square blocks, including the old Gayoso Hotel building.

Courtesy of Goldsmith's

The National Bisquit Company had offices on South Front Street in the early 1900s. This picture was taken about 1908. In Memphis, they manufactured crackers and candy. The company's name was later changed to Nabisco. It was incorporated in New Jersey in 1899. The Memphis operations moved to Florida Street, where a bakery was operated until the late 1940s. The location served as a distribution point until 1953 when the present Latham Street warehouse was opened.

Courtesy of Audrey and Harry Osborn

The warehouse of the John A. Denie's Sons Co., on Adams, photographed about 1912. This warehouse was purchased from the Southern Railway System, which had used it for a freight depot. During the Civil War, it was reportedly used as a barracks for troops.

Courtesy of John A. Denie's Sons Co.

D. Canale & Co., founded in 1866. This picture was
taken about 1910.

Courtesy of John D. Canale

The C. M. Callis Cheap Cash Store was on the southwest corner of Bridge and Cross Streets in Germantown. This picture was taken in August of 1912.

Courtesy of Harry Cloyes

This 1900 photograph shows one of the first apartment houses in Memphis, the Alcazar, at the corner of Adams and Fourth. It is no longer standing. Nationally, the first apartment houses were built by Rutherford Stuyvesant in New York in the 1870s.

Courtesy of Memphis Room, MASPLIC

Looking north on Front from Madison. On the left is the Illinois Central Station. As early as March of 1860, a street railway company began laying down tracks on Main Street for Memphis' first mule-car system. In 1891, two Chicagoans bought the system and modernized it. The change to electric lines, as a by-product, provided electricity for street lights. The Memphis Street Railway, by 1908, operated 120 to 160 cars daily on 109 miles of track, carrying an average of ninety-five thousand passengers per day.

Courtesy of Memphis Transit Authority

Election day for the Business Men's Club in April 1911. The club was founded in 1900 to promote investment in Memphis. In 1913, it affiliated with the United States Chamber of Commerce.

Courtesy of Memphis Room, MASPLIC

This young man, probably an electrician's helper, worked on motors in a shop of the Memphis Street Railway Co. The calendar girl, either early movie star Maxine Elliott, the "girl with the midnight eyes," or a lookalike, brightened the scene.

Courtesy of Memphis Transit Authority

Looking northeast on Main at Madison about 1903, at the beginning of a parade. The corner building was the later location of Walgreen's Drug Store.

Courtesy of Robert Ledbetter

Looking south on Main at Washington. The D. T. Porter Building and the Memphis Trust Building are down the street on the left. The street is torn up for laying of new tracks, circa 1905.

Courtesy of Memphis Transit Authority

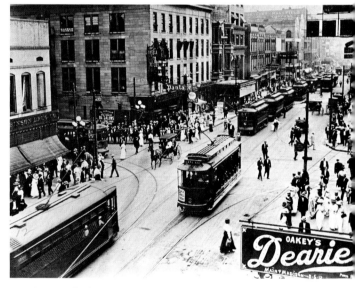

At the intersection of Main and Madison, looking north, in 1905. By 1912 the same intersection, looking south, was in heavy use.

Courtesy of Memphis Transit Authority
Courtesy of Bert Odessa Wade

Both pictures were taken of Main at Union looking north, the before picture in 1905, the after in 1912. The store to the right in both pictures is the same. By 1912, Julius Goodman had bought his father's interest in the diamond business.

Courtesy of Memphis Transit Authority
Courtesy of Bert Odessa Wade

The Memphis river front in 1907.

Courtesy of Memphis District,
Army Corps of Engineers

In 1910, Edward Hull Crump was elected mayor. It was the beginning of the Crump Era, which lasted until his death in 1954. Boss Crump controlled a political machine that ran both city and county and was a force in state and national politics as well. Wearing his inevitable carnation, he fought crime and corruption and pushed his commission form of government. Many Memphians refer to him as a benevolent dictator. In the car, left to right, are Crump's chauffeur Sidney, Tom Phillips, Marlin Speed, Crump, Leo Goodman, and John R. Riechman.

Courtesy of E. H. Crump, Jr.

Boss Crump, right, with J. W. Hale, in the late 1940s or early 1950s. By then his visage had mellowed. He took orphans on boat rides and wouldn't miss a football game, but his political power was as formidable as ever.

Courtesy of Memphis Room, MASPLIC

A division of the Memphis Police Department in the early 1900s.

Courtesy of Memphis Police Department

By the time the twentieth century began, the Memphis Police Department had grown from one constable appointed in 1827 to deal with Indian bands and flatboatmen, to a relatively sophisticated agency of law enforcement engaged in controlling gambling and prostitution. The first policemen depended heavily on citizens to help out when there was trouble, and they carried large rattles that doubled as clubs to signal for aid. In 1852 they got stars as police badges.

Courtesy of Memphis Police Department

The first patrol wagon, called the Black Maria, was put into use in the 1890s. The station moved in 1894 from Adams and Second to a tin-roofed, two-story converted cotton warehouse on Second at Washington, the location of this picture in the early 1900s. The rest of the Adams block, south to November Sixth Street, was enclosed by a high brick wall. Behind it, both male and female convicts worked out their sentences pounding rocks.

Courtesy of Memphis Police Department

The early 1900s were a time of transition for the police force in the area of transportation. In 1910, the first automobiles were bought: two Nationals, one for a patrol wagon, the other for an ambulance. Bicycles were tried in 1917, but the officers balked. These men were photographed on their motorcycles about 1915. The carnation was an important part of their dress uniform.

Courtesy of Memphis Police Department

Water wagons were used to keep the dust down on
city streets. They were filled at fire hydrants, then
sprinklers on the sides and in back watered the street.
This one stopped under a gas street lamp at
Watkins and Jefferson in 1907. The gas lamps, installed
on city street corners in the 1850s, were lit each night
by a man who traveled by bicycle to each one,
with a small ladder perched on his shoulders.

Courtesy of Bert Odessa Wade

Engine Company Number Three, on South Fourth Street (formerly DeSoto Street) after delivery of the new nickel-plated brass Nott steam fire engine in 1906.

Courtesy of Memphis Fire Department

The Nott engine saw action soon after its arrival. It pumped eight hundred gallons per minute. In 1976 the engine was taken out of storage to greet the American Bicentennial Freedom Train.

Courtesy of Memphis Pink Palace Museum

The Federal Building on Front Street, made of white Tennessee marble, was constructed in the 1890s. This view, taken April 6, 1905, shows the mail loading platform.

Courtesy of Memphis Post Office

The city scales, south of the Cossitt library, were surrounded by broken crates and old wagons in the early 1900s. A lot of the riverfront area was filled with debris until the community took measures to improve it.

Courtesy of Bert Odessa Wade

Memphian Henry Frank posed on an elaborate tricycle for a picture at Gray's Studio in 1905. His grandfather, Henry Frank, a Memphis cotton factor, lent his name to the steamer *Henry Frank,* a Mississippi steamboat that in 1870 carried the world's record cotton cargo. The tricycle's front wheel could be reversed and the contraption pulled like a wagon.

Courtesy of Memphis Room, MASPLIC

Union Station, Main and Calhoun, was built in 1912
at a cost of three million dollars. The eight-story
building had ten tracks and served the Illinois Central,
the Yazoo & Mississippi Valley, the Frisco, and Rock
Island lines. Despite protest from historical societies
and availability of government funds for its
preservation, the building was demolished in the late
1960s.

Courtesy of Memphis Room, MASPLIC

This was originally the Collier Building, completed in 1889 at a cost of 150 thousand dollars. It was located at Main and Jefferson and had the first elevator in Memphis. According to a newspaper account, a Mr. Gantt of the law firm Gantt & Patterson was selected to make the first trip by elevator, and a crowd gathered to cheer his safe landing. The building in 1892 was the headquarters of the *Memphis Appeal*, the newspaper that had packed up its presses and left Memphis just ahead of Federal occupation and stayed one step ahead of the Union Army throughout the war, publishing a strong Confederate paper all the while. The *Memphis Appeal* was the forerunner of the modern *Commercial Appeal*.

Courtesy of Memphis Room, MASPLIC

West Tennessee State Normal School opened
September 15, 1912. In this picture, the first summer
school students posed on the steps of the
Administration Building. In 1925 the school's name
was changed to West Tennessee State Teachers
College, in 1941 to Memphis State College, and in
1957 to Memphis State University.

Courtesy of Memphis State University

Fashionable Memphis women wore shirtwaists and hats, their waists cinched with corsets, on the porch of a downtown residence in 1905. Shirtwaists, which first appeared in the 1890s, could be ordered from Sears, Roebuck & Co. in 1905, in 150 versions, starting at thirty-nine cents. Hats were adorned with feathers, ribbons, lace, and silk flowers.

Courtesy of Mr. and Mrs. S. Nelson Castle

Woman's suffrage was long an issue in Tennessee. A limited bill was introduced in the State Senate as early as 1883. Later, the Memphis Equal Suffrage League was formed. In 1906, the Southern Woman Suffrage Conference was held in the city, and in 1914, the two Memphis groups held a rally in Court Square. In these pictures, women paraded in downtown Memphis for "whatsoever things are just," namely the vote. The "preparedness" banner carried by a group in one picture probably espoused readiness for United States entry into World War I, as preparedness parades were held all over the state at the time.

Courtesy of Memphis Pink Palace Museum

This photograph was taken by Milton Chick, a soldier at Park Field (Millington), about 1916.

Courtesy of Memphis Pink Palace Museum

The Forrest Rifles in 1907.

Courtesy of Memphis Pink Palace Museum

Officers of the Second Infantry, National Guard, Tennessee, at Camp Chickamauga, Georgia, August of 1908. Chickamauga means "river of death." The Confederates, under Bragg, emerged victor in the battle here that included one of the bloodiest single days of the Civil War. Historians say that if Bragg had moved quickly, he could then have taken Chattanooga.

Courtesy of Memphis Pink Palace Museum

The United Confederate Veterans Reunion, May 1901, was the largest ever held. A Confederate hall to hold eighteen thousand was built, and the city was decorated with fifteen thousand Confederate flags. Generals Fitzhugh Lee, Joe Wheeler, and John B. Gordon led the parade of fifteen thousand Civil War survivors. At a given spot, the parade took two and a half hours to pass. Many Memphians opened their homes to the veterans after all hotel space was taken. This ribbon, bearing a picture of General Nathan B. Forrest, commemorated the reunion.

Courtesy of Dr. Roland Bill

President William McKinley was welcomed in Court Square by Governor Benton McMillen and Mayor Joe Williams on April 30, 1901. President McKinley had been invited for the Confederate Veterans Convention, but a conflict of dates prevented his attendance and he came just before. Later, he dined on oysters, teal duck, and lobster cutlets at the Peabody Hotel with prominent Memphians and such notables as John Jacob Astor and Stuyvesant Fish.

Courtesy of Memphis Pink Palace Museum

After Admiral Dewey's victory over the Spanish at Manila Bay, he was honored all over the country. A committee of Memphians traveled by rail to Washington, D.C., to invite him to the city, and he accepted, arriving May 5, 1900. Admiral and Mrs. Dewey are shown here in the flower parade on the way to the reviewing stand.

Courtesy of Memphis Pink Palace Museum

At Main and Madison, banners bearing the likeness of Theodore Roosevelt lined the street in 1907. The traditional cotton arch waited in readiness for the inevitable parade. Roosevelt visited Memphis twice during his presidency. The first time, prominent Memphians invited him to a banquet in honor of General Luke E. Wright, whom President McKinley had appointed to the Philippine Commission. In 1907 he came for the Waterways Convention and expressed the Federal government's support of inland waterway development. "Fourteen feet through the valley" was the convention slogan.

Courtesy of Mrs. Oscar F. Blomberg

Golfers in front of Memphis Country Club about
1916. The inset shows a member on the greens. In
1898, a golf champion had come to Memphis to teach
beginners. By 1900 instruction in golf was considered
an important part of a young lady's education.

Courtesy of Mr. and Mrs. S. Nelson Castle

Before baseball, the only sport that got serious newspaper coverage was horse racing. But baseball soon became as popular with sportswriters as it was with the public. Teams cropped up all over Memphis in the 1870s. One of the first ball fields was Citizens Park, on the site of the Memphis Street Railway buildings at Beale and Walnut. And not far away, at Gallina's Saloon on Beale Street, Memphis' first professional team was organized in the 1880s. In 1901, a new league was formed, and the Memphis players, named the Turtles, won the pennant in 1903 and again in 1904, the year Harry McIntire pitched ten shutouts.

In the early 1900s, another team was formed called the Chicks, composed of young members of Memphis society. They were good players and popular with the public. People argued that they might be better than the Turtles, and subsequently a game was arranged, a great social event. The Turtles won, but the Chicks became a legend, and a few years later the Turtles adopted their name.

These two ball players and friends posed for a picture around 1910.

Courtesy of Memphis Transit Authority

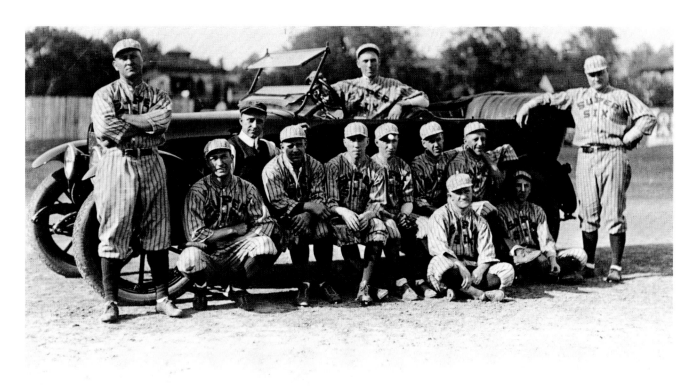

The Super Six baseball team.
Courtesy of Memphis Pink Palace Museum

A 1912 view of Main Street. A sign on the streetcar
advertises baseball at four p.m.

Courtesy of Bert Odessa Wade

Montgomery Park, later site of the fairgrounds, was
built by Henry Montgomery in the early 1880s for
thoroughbred racing. The Tennessee Derby originated
here in 1884. It attracted visitors from all over the
country until 1905, when the General Assembly
outlawed betting in Tennessee, and the park could no
longer attract the Grand Circuit. This photo was
taken about 1900.

Courtesy of Mrs. Oscar F. Blomberg

Memphis Driving Park, at Thomas and Firestone
Streets, was used for harness racing in the early 1900s.

Courtesy of Memphis Pink Palace Museum
Courtesy of Robert Ledbetter

The North Memphis Driving Park finish line, about
1900.

Courtesy of Memphis Room, MASPLIC

Whitehaven was named for Colonel Frank White, a president of the Mississippi & Tennessee Railroad and an early resident. He provided land for the first school there, the Whitehaven Academy, in 1885. This photo of its student body was taken around the turn of the century.

Courtesy of Anna Leigh McCorkle

A motorboat skims the river's surface about 1910.

Courtesy of Robert Ledbetter

The Christian Brothers High School Football team about 1913. The coach was Mr. Tyler "Fatty" McLean, who later became attorney general for Shelby County. The inset shows the team in action against Central High School.

Courtesy of Robert Ledbetter

The old Hernando Road, now Elvis Presley Boulevard. The road, named for Hernando de Soto, led from Memphis to Hernando, Mississippi. It is believed buffalo first made it and Indians used it long before white men came to West Tennessee.

Courtesy of Catharine Richey Hinton

G. F. Farrow, photographed in 1905, owned a stock farm in the country, on land which is now the business district of Whitehaven. His father, Lemuel Farrow, bought his land in the 1840s.

Courtesy of Catharine Richey Hinton

The J. W. Hale & Son store at Shelby Drive and Elvis Presley Boulevard, the only store in Whitehaven at the time, about 1900.

Courtesy of Catharine Richey Hinton

Most of Whitehaven in the early 1900s was farmland. There was time for sitting under an umbrella in the shadow of the smokehouse or riding through fields in an open wagon, shyly posing for the camera. And the big city of Memphis, only a couple of hours away by horse and carriage, offered many delights. A Whitehaven girl wrote in her journal of a trip to Memphis to hear John Philip Sousa in 1894, how they waited outside afterward to catch a glimpse of him, and how fine looking he was. She described with excitement the opening of the Raleigh Inn, with electric lights throughout, and how she was scandalized that a young man wanted to smoke in her presence.

Around World War II, Whitehaven's phenomenal growth began. Its farms were subdivided, an aluminum plant was built to make airplane parts, and it was later annexed to the City of Memphis.

Courtesy of Anna Leigh McCorkle
Courtesy of Catharine Richey Hinton

In the early 1900s several Whitehaven girls formed a group called the Whitehaven Walking Club. They gathered at Hale's store for afternoon walks. Members of the group later formed the Kennedy Book Club, a Whitehaven club still meeting in the 1970s.

Courtesy of Catharine Richey Hinton

The Wright brothers were successful with the first flight in 1903, but it wasn't until World War I, when planes were needed by the military for scouting and combat, that much progress was made in practical aviation. This biplane flew over Memphis with "Men Needed for the Air Service" painted on the underside of its wings. Many Memphis men did serve as pilots in World War I, probably because Park Field (now Millington Naval Air Station), the most important training camp in Tennessee during the war, was engaged principally in training plane commanders.

Courtesy of Memphis Pink Palace Museum

This picture recorded Memphis' first aerial mail service, December 7, 1918. Transcontinental airmail service began two years later. The plane is a Curtis Jennie.

Courtesy of Memphis Post Office

Glenn Curtis, the airplane manufacturer and innovator, demonstrates one of his early biplanes during a Memphis air show.

Courtesy of Memphis Pink Palace Museum

Two Curtis Jennies with the Signal Corps insignia. When World War I arrived, the Signal Corps became the Air Service, the forerunner of the Air Force. These planes were used to train pilots at Park Field.

Courtesy of Memphis Pink Palace Museum

These Navy bi-wing seaplanes docked at Memphis in the shadow of two large riverboats. The planes, from an Atlantic Coast squadron, had completed the first transatlantic flight, May 23, 1919. The trip took twenty-three days. Actual flying time was fifty-four hours. The pilots were entertained at a banquet with the Memphis Aero Club.

Courtesy of Memphis Pink Palace Museum

An aerial view of Memphis about 1915. The two streets in the foreground are Union and Monroe. The Napoleon Hill home stands at Third and Madison.

Courtesy of Memphis Pink Palace Museum

Union at Main, looking south, about 1912. Two billboards advertise Old North Street tobacco and the F. W. Cook Brewing Co.

Courtesy of Memphis Pink Palace Museum

Madison at Front, looking east, in 1912. F. M.
Guthrie, justice of the peace and notary public,
according to the advertisement in this picture, became
probate court judge in 1917.

Courtesy of Bert Odessa Wade

The intersection of Madison and Belvedere in 1912.
Courtesy of Bert Odessa Wade

Main at Court about 1918. The D. T. Porter Building is on the left.

Courtesy of Memphis Pink Palace Museum

The James T. Harahan Bridge, built upstream from
the Frisco Bridge, opened July 14, 1916. Plans for a
big celebration were interrupted by the United States'
entry into World War I. The bridge was named for
James T. Harahan, the Illinois Central Railroad
president killed in a train wreck in 1912. The first
automobiles crossed the Harahan in 1917 on a
wooden trestle. The first real highway bridge didn't
open until 1949.

Courtesy of Bert Odessa Wade

Floods

Memphis towers fifty feet above the highest water level ever reached by the Mississippi. But despite its enviable position, Memphis, too, has had the Mississippi's flood waters to contend with. A small area of the city to the north, near Bayou Gayoso, is subject to floods, and Memphis has cared for thousands of flood refugees from surrounding lowlands.

Until 1879 and the establishment of a Mississippi River Commission, the construction of levees was considered a local problem. The Commission could help in flood prevention, if those efforts were compatible with improvement of navigation. In 1927, one of the worst floods in history resulted in the passage of a flood control act calling for increased expenditure of federal funds. The river is now relatively under control, but Memphis still remembers high water. In 1937, more than fifty thousand flood refugees crossed the Harahan Bridge into Memphis, and cotton, taken from low-lying warehouses, was stacked high on Front Street.

These pictures, part of the Memphis Pink Palace Museum collection, show Memphis during the flood of April 1912.

A stranded wagon on Main Street.

A freight train at the rear of Gayoso Oil Works.

A flooded bridge in North Memphis. A walkway was
soon constructed on the side.

Near the gas works.

Market Street landing.

Dyking and pumping on Poplar. One of the first Mr. Bowers' stores is on the right. Memphis High School's towers are visible farther down the street.

The levee on Poplar, built by the Memphis Street Railway Co.

Within a few days the water had receded.

Refugees from Arkansas and Mississippi lowlands were cared for at the Tri-State Fairgrounds.

In the 1937 flood, portions of Riverside Drive were under water.

Courtesy of Memphis Room, MASPLIC

This picture was taken inside the Patterson Bayou Tunnel, built for prevention of floods in April 1920.

Courtesy of Mississippi Valley Collection
Memphis State University Libraries

In 1911, the city bought the former race track
Montgomery Park as home for the Tri-State Fair.
Here, its lights lure Memphians to an evening of fun.

Courtesy of Robert Ledbetter

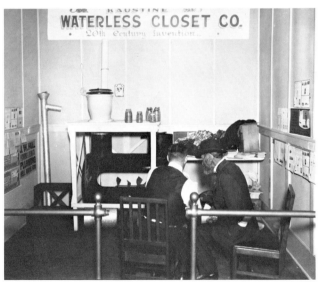

The Waterless Closet Co. demonstrated its product in
1918 at the fair. In 1880, only one home in six in the
city had indoor plumbing.

Courtesy of Memphis Room, MASPLIC

In 1918 one of the attractions of the fair was "Over the Falls." The cost was ten cents and a sign by the barker proclaimed "society attends."

Courtesy of Memphis Room, MASPLIC

A model displays three air-cooled Franklins at a
booth for the Dixie Motor Sales Co. in 1918. The
cars, a touring car and a roadster, featured electric
headlights and the new air-cooled engine.

Courtesy of Memphis Room, MASPLIC

The Memorial Circle of King's Daughters sold candy
for five cents at the fair, 1918.

Courtesy of Memphis Room, MASPLIC

154

The Navy and Marines recruited at the fair in 1918. Navy recruiting headquarters were at Main and Union streets, the Marines, at Main and Court in the Odd Fellows Building. In several months, Germany would sign an armistice heralding the end of the First World War.

Courtesy of Memphis Room, MASPLIC

United States Army recruiting at the fairgrounds, 1918. The Selective Service Act had gone into effect in May of 1917, requiring all men between the ages of twenty-one and thirty to register for military service. Later it was extended to eighteen and forty-five. Of the eighty thousand Tennesseans who saw service in the war, approximately twenty thousand were volunteers.

Courtesy of Memphis Room, MASPLIC

World War I

An Army lieutenant photographed at Park Field in December of 1917.

Courtesy of Memphis Pink Palace Museum

Memphians were outraged at Germany's aggressions. Feelings were at a fever pitch before the entry of the United States into the First World War. Twenty thousand Memphis men marched in a preparedness parade, and a few even went to Canada to join the British forces. After three American ships were sunk, including the *City of Memphis,* and the United States Congress declared war against Germany, thousands from the state volunteered for duty. Most of the 7,065 Tennessee guardsmen called to service became part of the Thirtieth Division, called "Old Hickory" for Andy Jackson.

In Memphis, the war interfered with the movement of the cotton crop, and, initially, unemployment was high. But people complained little and turned their efforts to supporting the war. Women and children raised victory gardens, people bought liberty bonds, and photographers went back to using glass negatives so as not to waste the raw materials of war.

Anti-German feeling was high. Schoolmasters ceased teaching the German language, and works by German composers were not played. Until the name of Germantown was changed to its Chickasaw name "Nashoba," meaning wolf, military troops threw mud balls at the Germantown station as their trains passed.

Three soldiers pose at a cannon in Confederate Park around 1915.

Courtesy of Memphis Pink Palace Museum

A Memphian in Army uniform around 1917.

Courtesy of Mr. and Mrs. S. Nelson Castle

Parts of a wrecked Air Service plane are moved on a New York Central flatcar to Park Field, accompanied by an Army guard.

Courtesy of Memphis Pink Palace Museum

A band made up of Park Field soldiers with mascot, circa 1915.

Courtesy of Memphis Pink Palace Museum

A soldier on a Front Street cotton scale, about 1915.

Courtesy of Memphis Pink Palace Museum

A Park Field pilot.

Courtesy of Memphis Pink Palace Museum

This soldier's motorcycle with side car carries the Air Service insignia on its tank. The picture was made about 1915. The opposite view of the same type of cycle is shown in the inset.

Courtesy of Memphis Pink Palace Museum

The 1919 Memphis Centennial parade had much to
celebrate. Memphis was one hundred years old, the
war was over, President Wilson had helped establish
the League of Nations, and the United States
unequivocally had become the greatest world power.

Courtesy of Memphis Pink Palace Museum

All the city-owned vehicles paraded for Memphis'
birthday. Here, water wagons joined the march.

Courtesy of Memphis Pink Palace Museum

A proud fire department shows off its fire wagon on
Main Street. Carnations had become an official part
of the city officials' dress uniform.

Courtesy of Memphis Pink Palace Museum

Confederate veterans in the Memphis Centennial
Parade, more than fifty years after the War Between
the States.

Courtesy of Memphis Pink Palace Museum

A woman soldier, a novelty at the time, on a parade
vehicle.

Courtesy of Memphis Pink Palace Museum

These women, either a Red Cross group or an early
female Navy or Marine detachment, are accompanied
by a male Army soldier.

Courtesy of Memphis Pink Palace Museum

Memphians performed a Centennial ceremony on the steps of the Court House. The Egyptian hand positions suggest that the dance was related to the city's namesake, Memphis on the Nile.

Courtesy of Memphis Pink Palace Museum

These cars were lavishly decorated for the parade.

Courtesy of Memphis Room, MASPLIC

A float for the Crippled Children's Hospital. The first children's hospital was opened in 1912 through the efforts of the Bachelors of Memphis, a group of young businessmen. In 1914, the city built the children's unit of City Hospital.

Courtesy of Memphis Pink Palace Museum

A group gets ready to photograph the parade at Adams and North Second Street in front of Calvary Episcopal Church. The man in clerical garb is probably Walter Davenport Buckner, who was minister of Calvary Episcopal from 1911 to 1920.

Courtesy of Memphis Pink Palace Museum

Main and Court about 1925, shortly after construction of the Columbia Mutual Tower, the white building on the corner. The buildings to its right housed the Ellis-Jones Drug Co. and the Railway Express Agency. In the lower left, street rails are being laid at Main and Jefferson.

Courtesy of Memphis Room, MASPLIC

From jubilation to Depression was a big step for any American city. Memphis soared in the 1920s and came down hard in the thirties. In the 1930 to 1940 decade, the city's growth rate was halved. The Fisher Body Co. of Memphis closed, putting 1,200 men out of work. Banks failed and businesses folded. But that was every city's story.

Locally, the period was not without its high points, especially when the twenties are included as a buffer. Memphis completed the first Municipal Airport in 1929. Many tall buildings were built downtown, including the twenty-two-story Lincoln American Tower and the thirty-one-story Sterick Building. Southern Presbyterian University (later Southwestern) located here. Several chain stores were started, and two chain restaurants made successful debuts. In 1934, Memphis voted for Tennessee Valley Authority power by an overwhelming majority, and Maiden Lane was renamed November Sixth Street to commemorate the day.

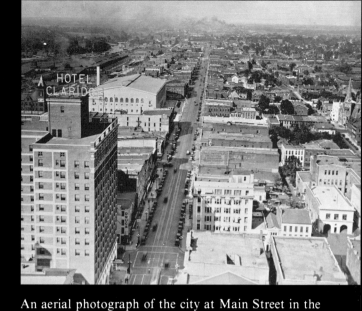

An aerial photograph of the city at Main Street in the 1920s. The auditorium and the Hotel Claridge had just been built.

Courtesy of Memphis Pink Palace Museum

The new Kress five-and-ten was built in 1927 on North Main. When S. H. Kress & Co. first opened in 1896, nothing in the store cost more than ten cents.

Courtesy of Walter Hughes

The first Peabody Hotel in Memphis was named for a Liverpool, England, man named George Peabody. He helped R. C. Brinkley get rails so the Memphis & Charleston could come to Memphis. The railroad was chartered in 1845, and in 1869, Brinkley built the Hotel Peabody at the northwest corner of Main and Monroe. It was the first steel framework building in Memphis. The Hotel Peabody pictured was built in 1925 on Union. Until its decline, it was one of the finest hotels in the South. In the 1960s, three million dollars were spent to revitalize it, but its doors were closed in 1975.

Courtesy of Memphis Room, MASPLIC

For a 1920s ball at the Peabody Hotel, debutantes were dressed to look like drinks. This girl represented a glass of champagne. It was one of many theme parties that season.

Courtesy of Scott Rightor Jacobs

The lobby of the Peabody Hotel featured rose and golden vein St. Genevieve marble. The fountain, usually filled with ducks, was black and gold travertine. Each night a porter escorted the ducks by elevator to the rooftop, where they slept.

Courtesy of Memphis Room, MASPLIC

The Hotel Claridge opened on Main Street in the 1920s.

Courtesy of Walter Hughes

In an office of Hughes Mechanical in the 1920s, the newest in home heating from the American Radiator Company was displayed.

Courtesy of Walter Hughes

Looking northwest on Poplar Avenue from the south
side of Overton Park in 1925.

Courtesy of Dr. Arlo Smith

A 1920s wedding party.

Courtesy of Scott Rightor Jacobs

Lieutenant Shea, Major Cuneo, and Lieutenant Donelson Lakes led the American Legion detachment in the Confederate Veterans Reunion parade, June 6, 1924.

Courtesy of Charles Aste, Jr.

In an Armistice Day parade in 1925, Memphians
Maury Jenkins, Robert Haverty, Lacey Whitten, Boyd
Wade, and Louis Carruthers were among those who
supported Billy Mitchell's contention that the Air
Service and the Air Force were superior to ships in
waging war. They had flown under him in France.
Many of these men, along with fellow Memphis Aero
Club members, founded Armstrong Field and were
instrumental in the development of the first municipal
airport.

Courtesy of Louis Carruthers

About 1920, this photograph was taken in front of
First United Methodist Church at Second and Poplar.
The church is one of the oldest in Memphis. It got its
charter even before the city did. It was started in a log
house with three members in 1826, and its first pastor
was Elijah Coffey, a Methodist circuit rider. This
greystone building was erected in 1889.

Courtesy of Memphis Pink Palace Museum

On the morning of July 10, 1929, a replica of the first
Memphis & Charleston train was met by the mayor
and citizens of Germantown in a re-enactment of the
1857 event which linked the Atlantic and the
Mississippi.

Courtesy of Harry Cloyes

A Germantown couple around 1930.

Courtesy of Harry Cloyes

A store in Germantown sold Blue Goose work shirts. Such businesses, family owned and run, would soon be replaced by large chains of discount stores.

Courtesy of Harry Cloyes

Clarence Saunders, in 1916, opened the first Piggly-Wiggly grocery store on Jefferson, between Front and Main. It featured self-service and a patented traffic flow pattern. Its prices were lower than the largest, most successful chain stores. It worked spectacularly well. In 1920, Saunders owned 515 Piggly-Wiggly stores, and by 1929 there were 2,500. Piggly-Wiggly had the highest sales per customer average of any grocery in the country. Saunders became a millionaire, then lost his money on the stock market. He again triumphed with a chain of Sole Owner of My Name stores; then the Depression ruined him. Several other ventures were moderately successful. He spent many years trying to develop new gimmicks in grocery merchandising, but none ever held the promise his self-service idea had.

Courtesy of Memphis Room, MASPLIC

In the 1920s, Clarence Saunders began building a twenty-two-room house of pink marble that he wanted to last for a thousand years. Cla-Lc-Clare, named for his three children, was to have an indoor swimming pool, ballroom, billiard room, and bowling alley. The grounds were to feature sunken gardens and a manmade lake fed by artesian wells. He had spent almost a million dollars on its construction when he lost his Piggly-Wiggly fortune. The city now owns the house, and developers divided the land to make Chickasaw Gardens. Memphis dubbed the house the Pink Palace, and the name stuck. The Memphis Pink Palace Museum is now housed in Cla-Le-Clare. The lake shown in this 1930s photo is gone and a modern building, a new addition to the museum, stands adjacent to it.

Courtesy of Memphis Room, MASPLIC

The Pink Palace Museum today.

Courtesy of Memphis Pink Palace Museum

Both Toddle Houses and Dobbs Houses got their start in Memphis in the 1930s. Toddle Houses, small ten-stool units, due to a labor shortage during World War II, had their customers pay by an honor system. Nationally, there were about 165 Toddle houses when Dobbs, an airline catering firm, bought them in 1962. This picture of the interior of a Toddle House reveals that hamburgers were once ten cents and steak plates forty cents.

Courtesy of Dobbs House

About 1930, the riverbank was strewn with trash. In the 1930s the area was graded and Riverside Drive constructed.

Courtesy of Memphis District,
United States Army Corps of Engineers

A view of Riverside Drive taken in 1940.

Courtesy of Memphis District,
United States Army Corps of Engineers

Prisoners at work at Shelby County Penal Farm in the 1930s. In 1917, the County Court Jail Commission agreed to the establishment of a correctional farm in lieu of building another conventional jail, but the Penal Farm wasn't a reality until much later. As an interim measure, in 1917, it was recommended the old jail be cleaned and disinfected and freshened by forced air currents.

Courtesy of Robert Ledbetter

In the twentieth century, goods are transported on the river on barges pushed by tugs.

Courtesy of Frank Garavelli

The Memphis Cotton Carnival was started in 1931 to promote cotton. It had its roots in the Mardi Gras celebrations instituted in the 1870s, but abandoned in the last major yellow fever epidemic. In this picture, the parade carries the carnival royalty down a downtown street that business has deserted.

Courtesy of Bert Odessa Wade

On a glowing barge, moving majestically down the Mississippi, the king and queen of cotton, the special princesses and ladies of the realm arrive to band music and a spectacular fireworks display. The Great River Pageant, the opening event of the Cotton Carnival, was photographed here in the late 1960s. Since 1931 the Cotton Carnival, steeped in mystery and tradition, has welcomed spring to the mid-South.

Courtesy of Memphis Area Chamber of Commerce

Main Street looking northeast from Madison during the Christmas season, about 1937.

Courtesy of Memphis Room, MASPLIC

Monroe looking west from Second Street November 1, 1931. Looming on the right are the Shrine Building, Lowenstein's, and the William Len Hotel.

Courtesy of Memphis Room, MASPLIC

In 1930 work was started on an addition to the Post
Office building on Front Street.

Courtesy of Memphis Post Office

From the year 1922 when they landed in Memphis broke after a barnstorming tour, Vernon and Phoebe Fairgraves Omlie were synonymous with flying in Memphis. Their first flying field was on the riverbank off North Second Street. From there, they went on to establish numerous aviation firsts. He flew the world's first forest fire patrol, gave E. H. Crump his first flight, helped organize the Memphis Aero Club, and flew political candidates around on what were probably the first aerial campaign tours. She was the first woman pilot in the United States to receive a license. She walked on wings and hung by her teeth and transferred from a moving plane to a moving auto. They formed the first Memphis flying school and helped establish Armstrong, the first Memphis municipal flying field.

In 1936, after Vernon Omlie was killed as a passenger in a plane crash, Phoebe Omlie served as air intelligence officer of the National Advisory Committee, Bureau of Air Commerce, but never flew again.

In this picture, Phoebe Omlie has just triumphed over fifty other aviators in an air derby from Santa Monica, California, to Cleveland, Ohio, in September of 1931.

Courtesy of Memphis Room, MASPLIC

The Omlies' flying circus performed all over the country. Phoebe, who weighed only ninety-five pounds, suffered several accidents, but as soon as the cast was off, she was flying again.

Courtesy of Robert Ledbetter

COMING TO PARMA, JULY 2=3
FREE! FREE!
IN CONNECTION WITH THE BIG PICNIC

This Plane Will Take Up Passengers At $5.00 A Ride

The World's Greatest:

Flying Circus!
With Miss Phoebe Fairgraves
American Premier Aviatrix

See her hang by her teeth; Stand on her head on top wing; Ride the tail of the ship; Hang by her toes from bottom wing; Loop on top while standing erect; Many other thrillers.

Southeast Missouri Oil Co's. Gas and Oil used in this exhibition

This Exhibition Staged By The Merchants and Business Men of Parma

THE PARMA PRESS PRINTERY

Beale Street

Courtesy of Memphis Room, MASPLIC

Beale was much more than a street. It was a legend every bit as grand as Bourbon Street in New Orleans or Peachtree Street in Atlanta. To Southern blacks it was a mecca. Beale Street had everything—adventure and danger and promise.

East on Beale were magnolia-laden lawns of the white upper class. As you went west toward the river, Beale diversified. There were saloons and theatres, bakeries, and an opera house, Church's Park, the Beale Street Baptist Church, Miss Higbee's School, a Chinese Masonic lodge. The businesses on Beale were owned primarily by Italians and Jews, but during the 1880s, a black middle class with interests in insurance, undertaking, banking, and restaurants emerged. One man, Robert R. Church, started with a saloon on Beale and became the first black millionaire in the South. A book published in 1908 listed sixty-five black Memphians with college degrees, seven of them women.

Beale was a dichotomy. It teemed with life, but life was nightly snuffed out in senseless slayings. A respectable place of commerce by day, it held pleasure and danger after dark.

Many people made up its legend. Harry Pace and W. E. B. Dubois edited *The Moon* there. W. C. Handy, already a popular band leader, came to Beale in 1905 and wrote "Memphis Blues" in Pee Wee's Saloon. Pee Wee arm wrestled his way to fame. He was also remembered for taking a swim across the Mississippi to the Arkansas shore on hot nights. Professor James Harris, Professor Love, West Dukes, Jim Turner, and Charlie Bynum all added to the music heritage of Beale Street, where they entertained in the Pastime, the first Beale Street theatre for blacks, and the Grand, and the Palace.

The dry laws of the early 1900s were little enforced on Beale Street. But in 1920, when prohibition became the law of the land, Beale Street's night life went underground. Organized underworld control of the vices became more embedded and more sinister.

In 1929, the Depression wiped out two black-owned Beale Street banks and consequently ruined many businesses. During World War II, Beale Street was off limits to all military personnel. Crackdowns and reforms made Beale clean and clear as a photographic plate wiped clean of emulsion. In the 1950s, television began to supplant moving pictures, and its theatres began to close. The civil rights movement of the 1960s brought new concerns and new opportunities to Memphis blacks, and Beale was forever gone.

The shells of buildings left don't say much about what they once contained. In the 1970s, the only things left were a store that sold voodoo candles, the old church, George Lee's Atlanta Life office, and the Hunt-Phelan home that General Grant occupied during the Civil War, surrounded by a high fence topped with barbed wire.

The Knights of Pythias Band, photographed in 1909 at Main and Madison. One of the most popular bands in Memphis, they were hired during a three-way race for mayor by supporters of a young reformer named E. H. Crump. A new tune, written by W. C. Handy (see arrow), caught on, and it became Crump's campaign song. "Mr. Crump don't allow no easy riders here. I don't care what Mr. Crump don't 'low, I'm gonna bar'l-house anyhow." The name was later changed from "Mr. Crump Blues" to "Memphis Blues." It was published in 1912, but Handy sold his rights to it to T. C. Bennett, then the head of Bry's Department Store's music department for fifty dollars. Soon after, Handy wrote the "St. Louis Blues," "Yellow Dog Blues," "Joe Turner Blues," and the others that made Handy and Beale Street famous and gave the blues to the world.

Courtesy of Harry E. Godwin

Beale Street, looking east, about 1915. On the right hand side of the street are the famous musicians' hangout, P. Wee's, where Handy wrote his blues, and Battier's Drugs. About the time this picture was taken, Abe Plough purchased the drugstore and launched his retail drug business, selling C-2223, a remedy for rheumatism, and Plough's Antiseptic Healing Oil. He had started manufacturing pharmaceuticals at the age of sixteen in a single room above his father's furniture store on North Second Street. Both Plough Chemical Company and Plough's Pantaze drugstores prospered. In 1931 a Memphis newspaper reported Abe Plough was insured for one-and-a-half million dollars.

Photo by Hooks Bros.

This LeMoyne Normal Institute class, taught by Emma Hatcher, was photographed about 1910. Among the students were Alabama Howard (to the right of the teacher), who grew up to teach at Geeter School; and Dan Fields (the tall one in the back) who later became the proprietor of Mt. Carmel Hollywood Cemetery. LeMoyne, founded in 1870, was the first school in Memphis for ex-slaves. Then, it consisted of a simple wood frame structure or Orleans, near Beale Street, that was built with money given by Dr. F. Julius LeMoyne, an eminent physician from Washington, Pennsylvania. LeMoyne became a four-year college in 1931 and the next year awarded eighteen degrees. It was merged with Owen Junior College in 1968.

Photo by Hooks Bros.

This Consolidated Liberator bomber was named *The Spirit of Beale Street* after Memphis blacks bought 303 thousand dollars in war bonds. Lieutenant George W. Lee headed the fund drive.

Photo by Hooks Bros.

William Christopher Handy bought his first cornet as a boy in Florence, Alabama, for $1.75. By the time this picture was taken in the 1940s, he was world famous for his blues. He had seen the possibilities in the primitive music that had begun in Southern cotton fields. He listened well and took its rhythmic strains and gave it back "on a silver platter...more beautiful."

Courtesy of Memphis Room, MASPLIC

Spontaneity and improvisation marked the music of Beale Street in its heyday. This unidentified jug band was photographed in Handy Park in 1949.

Courtesy of Harry E. Godwin

Sun Smith learned the trumpet at a school for the blind in Nashville. In Memphis, in the thirties and forties, he played with Frank Stokes, Will Batts, Gus Cannon, and Handy, and helped start the Citizens Club, a famous Beale Street nightclub. His band, Sun Smith's Beale Street Five, is now led by Charlie Banks. When Sun Smith died in 1976, his friends organized a blues funeral.

Courtesy of Harry E. Godwin

She sang "Bumblebee Blues" and "Black Rat Swing" and blues fans loved it. Memphis Minnie (Minnie Lawler) was born in 1900 in Algiers, Louisiana. After she had a stroke in 1960, she could never sing again. An English girl who loved her music sent Memphis blues promoter Harry Godwin $113.75 she had raised in a concert, and Godwin, Furry Lewis, and Joe Dobbins presented it to Minnie along with a special concert at the nursing home. This photograph was taken in 1968.

Photo by Dr. F. Jack Hurley

The Randolph House, typical of those that lined the east end of Beale in the late 1800s. The building and a carriage house in back were torn down in 1976 after a fire had gutted the house's interior.

Courtesy of Memphis Room, MASPLIC

Walter "Furry" Lewis, one of the most famous blues guitarists in the world, photographed in 1967. Born in Greenwood, Mississippi, in 1893, he moved to Memphis as a child. He is a master of the bottleneck style of guitar playing, named so because guitarists used to break a bottle and use the neck on the strings for a glissando effect. Furry Lewis was featured in the movie *W. W. & the Dixie Dance Kings* with Art Carney and Burt Reynolds in 1974 and has played in Madison Square Garden. Back in the 1930s, in Philadelphia, he participated in the first United States blues festival ever held.

Photo by Dr. F. Jack Hurley

Beale at Second Street in the 1960s. The tall building on the far side of the street is the M & M Building. Originally called the Randolph Building, it was the first high rise structure in the city. It was built of wood frame construction before the turn of the century.

Courtesy of Memphis Housing Authority

George Washington Lee, shown here on Beale Street with Marva Louis (Joe Louis' first wife). His book, *Beale Street,* published in 1934, was a Book-of-the-Month Club selection. In the 1970s, he was one of the few businessmen left on Beale. Known for his eloquence and his loyalty to the Republican party, he was elected as a delegate to the Republican National Convention in 1976 at the age of eighty-two, but died in a car accident a few weeks before the event.

Courtesy of George W. Lee

A Memphis radio station sold defense bonds and
stamps during World War II.

Courtesy of Memphis Room, MASPLIC

1940-1976

In 1820 or 1920, if you took a photograph of downtown Memphis, perhaps including a bit of the Mississippi River, you'd get a representative photograph, something to frame and call Memphis. But in ensuing decades the city has changed. Main Street isn't Main Street anymore. The city has moved east and what was once its main artery is the new Mid-America Mall, dedicated in 1976, an attraction, but not the vital center it was in the past.

World War II was the catalyst for change. In the 1940s, twenty new industries, as well as Second Army Headquarters, moved here, and a gigantic Army hospital was built. The Memphis-Arkansas Bridge opened and a city expressway was started. The I-40 interchange was halted, though, at the edge of Overton Park when citizens protested invasion of the park by a highway.

In October of 1954, when Edward Hull Crump died, central government control also died. In the 1970s political power was divided and the black community sent its first congressman to Washington.

The population, 292,942 in 1940, was 667,150 in 1975. Memphis ranked seventeenth in population among United States cities.

This aerial view shows the many buildings of Kennedy General, built in 1943 as an Army hospital. The name was changed to Veterans Administration Medical Teaching Group Hospital in 1946. The area was bounded by Park on the north, Quince on the south and Hiawatha on the east. It covered 150 acres. Its western boundary was Shotwell Road, but after the hospital was built, the name was changed to the more appropriate Getwell. The land now belongs to Memphis State University. A new Veterans Administration hospital was built at Jefferson and Pauline in 1967.

Courtesy of Veterans Administration Hospital

The riverfront in the 1940s.

Courtesy of Scott Rightor Jacobs

The pavilion in Overton Park around 1900. The inset
shows the log cabin on the small island to the left in
the larger picture. The area became the Japanese
Gardens, and a bridge was built connecting the small
island to the shore.

Courtesy of Robert Ledbetter

The Japanese Gardens at Overton Park. They were removed from the park during World War II when sentiment against the Japanese was strong.

Courtesy of Memphis Room, MASPLIC

The Japanese Gardens during a rare snow. The apparent smoke is actually due to a damaged glass negative.

Courtesy of Memphis Room, MASPLIC

In March of 1948, the steamer *Sprague* made her last trip with eight empty oil barges before decommissioning, after forty-six years on the Mississippi. She once carried the largest tow on the river.

Courtesy of Frank Garavelli

The *Argonaut,* a modern riverboat, boasts 10,500 horsepower.

Courtesy of Frank Garavelli

Looking south on Main from Monroe in the early 1940s. At the Warner Theatre, Humphrey Bogart, Alexis Smith, and Sidney Greenstreet star in *Conflict*. Commerce Square now occupies the theatre site.

Courtesy of Memphis Room, MASPLIC

Missouri Pacific Locomotive Number 9472 was used by the Memphis Union Station engine house. This photo was taken by John E. Martin in June of 1940.

Courtesy of Memphis Room, MASPLIC

Ice floes formed on the Mississippi during a rare period of extreme cold in the winter of 1956-57.

Photo by Tom Wofford

THE REBEL YELL THAT WAS HEARD 'ROUND THE WORLD

When Barbara Jo Walker won the Miss America contest in 1947, *Commercial Appeal* cartoonist Cal Alley depicted a proud Colonel Memphis emitting "the rebel yell heard round the world." She is to date the only Tennessee contestant ever to hold the title.

Courtesy of Barbara Walker Hummel

Federal Express Corp., founded in 1972 by Memphian Frederick Smith, started out with one plane and six packages and has grown to an airline of thirty-three fan jets carrying over twenty thousand packages nightly.

Courtesy of Federal Express Corp.

In 1952 Kemmons Wilson opened the first Holiday Inn in Memphis on Summer Avenue. The Memphis-based company now owns motels all over the world. The Summer Avenue motel shown still exists, but it has been sold and the name changed.

Courtesy of Holiday Inns, Inc.

The north end of Ellis Auditorium before construction of the convention center. On the other side of Ellis, at Washington and Adams, soldiers from Millington were dropped off at the bus stop for a night on the town. During the 1950s, the street was lined with locker clubs, uniform shops, and Army surplus stores.

Courtesy of Memphis Housing Authority

The Everett R. Cook Convention Center adjoins the old Ellis Auditorium across Exchange Street. The center, completed in 1973 to accommodate twenty-five thousand, was named for Everett R. Cook, a World War I fighter pilot, Deputy Chief of Staff of the Eighth and Twelfth Air Forces in World War II, and founder of the Memphis-based Cook Industries, Inc.

Courtesy of Memphis Area Chamber of Commerce

An Ole Miss-Memphis State football game opened the Memphis Liberty Bowl Stadium in 1965. It was built on a former gravel yard adjacent to the fairgrounds on South Hollywood.

Courtesy of Memphis Area Chamber of Commerce

In 1955, the Memphis Academy of Art built the structure pictured in Overton Park. It was the prize-winning design of architects Roy Harrover and Bill Mann. The Academy, incorporated in 1936, was initially housed in the Board of Education building on Adams Avenue. They later moved to the historic Lee home. In the 1970s, the school was granting 250 degrees per year and holding classes for seven hundred special students.

Courtesy of Memphis Academy of Art

This picture recorded Memphis State's jubilation at gaining university status in 1957. In the center is J. Millard Smith, Memphis State president from 1946 to 1960.

Courtesy of Memphis State University

In the spring of 1968 the city sanitation workers went on strike for union bargaining and deduction of union dues from workers' paychecks. For ten weeks and twelve days the strike lasted. Mayor Loeb refused to give in, but by city council resolution the contract was signed.

Courtesy of Mississippi Valley Collection
Memphis State University Libraries

In 1960 Danny Thomas founded Saint Jude Children's Research Hospital in Memphis. Here, he is shown with Fred Gattas, one of the hospital's original board members.

Photo by Saul Brown

After Martin Luther King was shot, April 4, 1968,
National Guardsmen lined the route of the Memorial
March at Beale and South Second.

Courtesy of Mississippi Valley Collection
Memphis State University Libraries

This view of Clark Tower was taken from White
Station Tower. The two skyscrapers, stragglers from
the city's skyline, were built in 1970 and 1966,
respectively, on Poplar Avenue.

Courtesy of Memphis Area Chamber of Commerce

In the 1970s Overton Square was developed at Madison and Cooper. Old buildings were converted into restaurants, theatres, and shops. The area now encompasses several blocks.

Photo by Mike Plunkett

In the spring of 1976, the Mid-America Mall was dedicated. This is a view of Main Street looking south.

Photo by Mike Plunkett

Deckhands aboard the *Delta Queen*, photographed in 1976. She has operated on the Mississippi since 1947. The *Delta Queen* was the last large passenger boat built until the *Mississippi Queen*, which got underway in May 1976.

Courtesy of Delta Queen Steamboat Co.

Elvis Presley at his 1974 Memphis concert. Born in Tupelo, Mississippi, in 1935, Elvis moved with his family to Memphis in 1949. In the 1950s, he toured with manager Colonel Tom Parker as "The Hillbilly Cat." Since his early successes, "Blue Suede Shoes" and "Hound Dog," he has become a legend and is lauded as the king of rock and roll. Daily, fans come in droves to gaze through the gate of his Graceland Mansion on the street Memphis named for him.

Photo by Gene Tuck

Over a million Memphians a year attend events in the twelve-thousand-seat Mid-South Coliseum, erected in 1964. It opened with the Ringling Brothers Circus. Elvis Presley's appearance at the coliseum in 1974 marked his first appearance in Memphis in over ten years.

Courtesy of Memphis Area Chamber of Commerce

The Hernando DeSoto Bridge, built to the north of the Frisco, the Harahan, and the Memphis and Arkansas, was completed in the 1960s. The quartet of Memphis-Arkansas bridges are Memphis' link to the West. The Hernando DeSoto, its arches forming a gigantic "M" on the Memphis side, was built to handle increased traffic and serve the interstate highway system. Before it was built, any bridge repairs on the Memphis and Arkansas cut off automobile traffic between the two states.

Courtesy of Memphis Area Chamber of Commerce